# A
# YIDDISH
# WORD BOOK
# FOR
# ENGLISH-
# SPEAKING
# PEOPLE

## SAMUEL ROSENBAUM

 **VAN NOSTRAND REINHOLD COMPANY**
NEW YORK    CINCINNATI    ATLANTA    DALLAS    SAN FRANCISCO
LONDON    TORONTO    MELBOURNE

Van Nostrand Reinhold Company Regional Offices:
New York   Cincinnati   Atlanta   Dallas   San Francisco

Van Nostrand Reinhold Company International Offices:
London   Toronto   Melbourne

Copyright © 1978 by Litton Educational Publishing, Inc.

Library of Congress Catalog Card Number: 77-20021
ISBN: 0-442-27015-1

Manufactured in the United States of America

Published by Van Nostrand Reinhold Company
450 West 33rd Street, New York, N.Y.   10001

Published simultaneously in Canada by Van Nostrand Reinhold Ltd.

15  14  13  12  11  10  9  8  7  6  5  4  3  2  1


Library of Congress Cataloging in Publication Data

Rosenbaum, Samuel.
    A Yiddish word book for English-speaking people.

    1. Yiddish language—Dictionaries—English.
2. English language—Dictionaries—Yiddish.  I. Title.
PJ5117.R65        437'.947        77-20021
ISBN 0-442-27015-1

*"To my parents,
Brayna and Itzik Rosenbaum,
who implanted in me
their love for Yiddish."*

# CONTENTS

## ABOUT YIDDISH

Yiddish, the mother tongue of generations of Jews of Eastern and Central Europe, has a history of over 800 years. Its core, the foundation on which it developed, is an old Germanic dialect. But it would be deceptive to believe that Yiddish is therefore no more than a variation on that dialect. Actually, no language has come down to us full-blown, original and pure from beginning to end. Strains of the very same German dialect from which Yiddish evolved can be easily detected in Swedish, Danish, Dutch, and in several other European tongues.

What uniquely distinguishes Yiddish from its core dialect are the accretions of Hebrew and bits and pieces of the languages of the countries in which the Jews found themselves over those eight centuries, particularly Russia and Poland.

Yiddish, the name of the language, derives from *yid,* Jew. In Yiddish, a Jew is called *a yid.* And as is its name, Yiddish is the language created and spoken by Jews and inseparably linked to Jewish life.

At the time of the onset of World War II, Yiddish was the primary language of the millions of Jews of Central and Eastern Europe. Hebrew was the language of prayer, Jewish scholars, and scholarship. It was also the language of the Jewish intellectuals, who in the late 19th century, began to enlarge Hebrew from its narrow confines as *losh'n koydesh* (the sacred tongue) to wider use in literature, journalism, and correspondence. Although some Hebrew was spoken in intellectual circles, it did not become a living language until it became the national language of the early settlers in Palestine, and later, in 1948, of the State of Israel.

Most linguists agree that Yiddish was, at its height of popularity—in the 1930s—70% German, 20% Hebrew, and 10% Slavic. Today, many of the Hebrew and Slavic words have gradually been discarded and replaced by words borrowed from English. It is quite common to hear, even from elderly speakers of Yiddish, the words *nekst-dorke*, lady next door or neighbor, instead of *sh'kheyne*, the Hebrew-root word. Or, *flor*, instead of *padloge*, the Slavic-root word for floor. Or, *vinde*, instead of the German-root, *fenster* for window.

How old is Yiddish?

The library of the Hebrew University in Jerusalem contains a manuscript of a prayer book in Yiddish dated 1272. The manuscript was created in Worms in the Rhine Valley. It was discovered after World War II and finally found its way to Jerusalem. Before the discovery of the manuscript, there were other Yiddish manuscripts which scholars judged to be from the 13th century, but none of these was dated and so the time of their origin was only an estimate. The next oldest dated Yiddish manuscript was discovered early in the 20th century in a hidden synagogue book storage room (*genizah*) in Cairo by the famous Cambridge scholar of Judaica, Solomon Schechter. It was dated 1382, and may now be found in the library at Cambridge. While Yiddish may not have been the most popular language of the Jews of Cairo in the 14th century, it is obvious that some Cairo Jews spoke or read Yiddish.

The difficulties under which Jews lived during the last 800 years made it imperative that Jews should develop a language with which they could communicate with fellow Jews all over the world, as easily as with Jews in the next village.

Because it was the language of the Bible, the Talmud, and the prayer book, Hebrew, the sacred tongue, could not serve this purpose. Most Jews did not understand Hebrew, except for the most commonly used prayer texts, although the majority could read it.

Spoken Yiddish became written Yiddish via the characters of the Hebrew alphabet. Strangely enough, those that developed Yiddish, spoke it, and wrote it, were not greatly enamored of it. They looked upon its use as a matter of necessity.

In the 19th century, when the European Jewish community was undergoing great social and philosophic transformations, there were those who felt that along with physical and social emancipation, Jews should be freed from what they believed to be the tyranny and superstitions of a religiously oriented lifestyle. They soon realized that they could reach the masses only in common, everyday Yiddish.

Even the early giants of Yiddish literature, Yitzkhok Leyb Peretz, Sholom Aleykhem, Mendele Moykher S'forim, wrote in Hebrew, until they realized that they were limiting their readership to a small minority of intellectuals. Only then, and only out of a practical need, did they begin to write in Yiddish. And only then did they become popular with the Jewish masses.

Students of early Yiddish literature maintain that Sholom Abramovitch and Sholom Rabinovitch became Mendele Moykher S'forim (Mendele, the Book Seller) and Sholom Aleykhem (Mr. How Do You Do) because they were embarrassed to speak in their own names and invented pseudonyms for folk-type narrators who spun out their stories of the everyday little people in their everyday language, Yiddish.

As with the Jewish people, each generation has had its prophets who forecast the imminent demise of Yiddish. Today, that is not too difficult a prophecy to substantiate.

Gone are the four or five great daily Yiddish newspapers which flourished in the first half of the 20th century, along with hundreds of thousands of their readers. Almost gone are the great publishers of Yiddish books in America, to say nothing of the giant publishing houses of Poland and Lithuania.

Practically extinct, too, is the Yiddish theater which played everything from Shakespeare to Sholom Asch. Except for an occasional production undertaken by a nonprofit Yiddish cultural organization, or a one-time plunge by a nostalgic producer whose motives are pure, but whose profits, if any, are microscopic, there is no longer a viable Yiddish theater in America today.

In its time the Yiddish theater was a great acculturational force for the immigrants who filled to overflowing the 25 or more theaters in the major Jewish cities like New York, Philadelphia, Boston, or Chicago. Except for the classics by gifted playwrights like Jacob Gordin, Peretz Hirshbein, or Aaron Zeitlin, almost all of the plays—with or without music—dealt with the transition from *shtetl* life to American life. (Life in a rural Jewish village in eastern Europe; *shtetl*, literally means little town.) It was the Yiddish theater that acquainted the immigrant with his first words in English thus contributing to the Americanization of Yiddish, and in a sense to its contamination, and to some extent, its demise. As soon as *di grine* (the green ones, the immigrants) learned English they gradually abandoned the Yiddish theater for American-style entertainment.

However, there were never more producing Yiddish poets and novelists than there are today. Although some may create in English, they do so in the spirit, rhythm, and even prosody of Yiddish. In the few decades since World War II, Yiddish seems to have been transformed from a language of the masses to an elitist tongue. This might be so except for one factor, the irrepressible love of the masses for *mame losh'n* (the mother tongue).

Anyone who is at all alert to the sociological developments of the last several decades must know of the more intense consciousness which minority groups, especially, have about their past, their traditions, and their culture. This is true of Jews, as well. While we have our problems with intermarriage, there are no more "closet Jews." This is not to say that Jews are necessarily more pious or observant or even care more about being Jews, but they are more aware of things Jewish and are not ashamed to identify with them and to use them. The immense popularity of the works of Sholom Aleykhem, I. B. Singer, Irving Howe, Philip Roth, and Saul Bellows with the general American public, and the fact that the writing establishment in the 1950s and 1960s was predominantly Jewish and wrote predominantly on their experiences as Jews, or on Jewish characters, is ample testimony to the reawakening of interest in Jews and their language of Yiddish. During the past four or five years, Yiddish speaking groups have sprung up on campuses all across the country. Literally hundreds of Yiddish words, e.g., *nudnik*, *shlep*, *khutspe*, etc. have filtered into contemporary English and now roll off the tongues of Wasps as easily as from the tongues of our *bobes* (grandmothers).

So, there is obviously an interest in Yiddish. The problem is that along with this growing interest in Yiddish and identification with Jewishness (which is not the same as Judaism), most Americans, Jews and others, alike, cannot read Yiddish.

This wordbook is intended primarily for those who would like to use Yiddish words and expressions in their conversation and correspondence with a full understanding of what they are saying, or what someone else is saying to them. It is the first and only transliterated Yiddish–English wordbook in the world and will be of interest not only to the American Jew but to non-Jews who may have business or social contacts with Jews. It will be of particular interest to college students who want to know Yiddish but for whom the task of learning to read Yiddish and becoming fluent in it is something which is still in the future.

The wordbook contains over 2000 Yiddish entries. These entries consist not only of the most common Yiddish words but of the most popular and useful folk expressions, idioms, and proverbs which can be heard in the Yiddish of literate Jews. There is also an English-Yiddish reverse section. Yiddish entries offer two, three, and even four alternate definitions giving different shadings of meaning. Each of these definitions constitutes a separate entry on the English side.

There are no capital letters in Yiddish, neither for proper names or places, nor at the beginning of a sentence; therefore, all entries—words, phrases, idioms, etc. —will be in lowercase.

In addition to knowing the language, one should know something about the cultural and religious life of the people, at least insofar as items which might come up in daily usage. We have, therefore, done more than transliterate words like *bar mitsve*, *bris*, or *khanuke*, etc. We have provided a concise explanation of what these events or occasions and all other similar entries mean in Jewish life. It should be helpful to someone invited to a *pidyon habeyn* to know more than the literal translation of the words. The wordbook, therefore, is also a useful encyclopedia of specifically Jewish religious and cultural items.

This brings us to the question of transliteration, spelling out a word in English in such a way as to permit one to pronounce the Yiddish properly. A problem arises due to the fact that there are many letter combinations that might represent the sound of Yiddish words.

Take, for instance, the well-known expletive of dismay: *oy vey*! or woe is me! It could, conceivably, be spelled *oi vay*, *oye veigh*, or any combination of several vowels. The reader will certainly be acquainted with the many ways of spelling the name of the Feast of Lights: Chanuka, Hanukkah, Chanookah, or Chanukoh.

To avoid confusion and to lend support to those Yiddish scholars who have struggled with this problem for decades, the Yiddish entries in this book will be spelled according to the YIVO* transliteration scheme which has been evolved by the acknowledged scholars in the field and which is recognized as definitive by all who are engaged in serious Yiddish scholarship.

The system is quite simple. All consonants are pronounced as they are in English. There are two additional consonants which do not appear in English, although they will be familiar to those acquainted with German: the guttural sound for the letter ח and כ, both of which are transliterated as *kh*. Thus Hanukkah, as it is most commonly spelled in "English" will be written in our transliteration as *khanuke*. The sound of *kh* is very similar to the *ch* in the German *ach* or *dich*.

There are, in Yiddish, some combinations of consonant sounds which are not usually found in English:

*zh*   as in seizure or pleasure
*ts*   as in rats or sits

Vowels are pronounced as follows:

*a*    as in ah
*ay*   as in my
*e*    as in bed; never silent, pronounced even when it is the final letter in a word
*ey*   as in day
*i*    as in bid (within a word)
*i*    as in bee (where it is the final or only letter in a word)
*o*    as in up
*oy*   as in boy
*u*    as in rule

There are five vowels in Yiddish (*a, e, i, o, u*) and one silent letter (א-alef).

*Acronym for *Yidish'n Visenshaftlekhen Institut*, Yiddish Scientific Institute, now known as YIVO Institute for Jewish Research.
YIVO, was founded in Wilno, Poland in 1925, for the study of Jewish life and history in all parts of the world, and particularly in eastern Europe. Through its program of research and publication it became an international center of Jewish scholarship and intellectual activity. By the time it was moved to New York, at the outbreak of World War II, it had already published a good number of scholarly works on history, philology, economics, folklore, and psychology. In addition, there were numerous works on Jewish history, the Yiddish language, literature, and theater.
In New York, YIVO continued its traditional activities while turning its attention increasingly to the study of Jewish life in America. Today, YIVO boasts an extraordinary Jewish library and probably the world's greatest archive on European Jewry.

## ABOUT THE WORDBOOK

Yiddish entries are divided into pronunciation syllables. An accent mark over a syllable indicates where the stress goes in pronunciation:

**be-héy-me    ba-le-bós    fén-ster**

Since so many of the Yiddish entries are words derived from the Hebrew or taken over bodily from the Hebrew, such entries will also contain the original Hebrew word in parentheses. However, in transliterating Hebrew into English, we have tried to conform to the common scholarly style for that language which differs somewhat from that used in Yiddish transliteration.

Before looking up a word or phrase in the Yiddish section, the reader should become familiar with the system used consistently throughout this book of spelling Yiddish words in English characters. The transliteration system is given above, as is a chart of special Yiddish vowels and consonants.

The idioms and phrase entries are usually translated literally and then given in an English setting which carries the same feeling, although it may bear no resemblance to the literal Yiddish. For example, *vi a yóv'n in sú-keh* is translated literally as: like a pagan in a hut (in which observant Jews live during the holiday of *súkes*, Festival of Booths). In English, we might convey the same idea with: like a bull in a china shop.

## ABOUT GRAMMAR

Since the wordbook is not a language method, but a vocabulary aid, we have kept grammatical information at a minimum. You may not care to become involved in the labyrinthian complexities of Yiddish grammar and will use the wordbook without recourse to rules of sentence structure, etc.

However, there will be some who will appreciate general information on the basic Yiddish parts of speech in order to be able to translate forms of the Yiddish entries other than the basic ones given in the wordbook. Such a smattering of grammar follows.

### Definite Articles

There are four forms for "the": *der* (masculine), *di* (feminine), *dos* (neuter), *di* (plural, for all genders).

Each noun entry is followed by the appropriate definite article. Again, as in most languages, there is no rule governing the gender of nouns. One must simply use them often enough together with the appropriate definite article and thus get to remember them:

> **be-héy-me** (*di*—feminine), domesticated animal
> **ba-le-bós** (*der*—masculine), boss, owner, landlord
> **fén-ster** (*dos*—neuter), window
> **hóy-z'n** (*di*—plural), trousers

## Indefinite Articles

> **a** (before consonants)
> **an** (before vowels)

The indefinite articles are not affected by the gender of the noun.

## Nouns

Noun entries are given in the singular, except such nouns are normally occur as a pair or as a collective group:

> **di shikh**, the shoes
> **di tseyn**, the teeth
> **di hóy-z'n**, the trousers

It will be helpful, in comprehending plural nouns, to be familiar with the several ways in which nouns form their plurals. As the reader will see, there is no hard and fast relationship between the gender of a noun and the way it forms its plural.

1. By adding *s*:
   > **der lér-er, di lér-ers**, teacher(s)
   > **der af́-bet-er, di af́-bet-ers**, worker(s)
   > **der zéy-ger, di zéy-gers**, clock(s)
2. By adding *n* or *en*:
   > **di oyg, di óyg-'n**, eye(s)
   > **di ban, di bán-en**, train(s)
   > **der taykh, di táykh-en**, river(s)
3. By adding *er*:
   > **dos bild, di bíld-er**, picture(s)
   > **dos kind, di kínd-er**, child, children
   > **der shteyn, di shtéyn-er** stone(s)

4. By adding *im*, and often with a  vowel change:*
       der khá-ver, di kha-vér-im, friend(s)
       der tál-mid, di tal-míd-im, pupil(s)
       der khéy-der, di kh'-dó-rim, room(s)
5. A change in vowel:
       der barg, di berg, mountain(s)
       der tog, di teg, day(s)
       di tókh-ter, di tékh-ter, daughter(s)
6. By adding *es*, and an occasional vowel change:
       der dor, di dóyr-es, generation(s)
       der kóy-akh, di kóyh-es, strength(s)
       der kóy-men, di kóy-men-es, chimney(s)
7. By adding *ekh*:
       der yíng-'l, di yíng-lekh, lad(s)
       di líkht, di líkht-lekh, candle(s)
       di méyd-'l, di méyd-lekh, girl(s)

There are a small number of additional plural forms but these are so irregular as to defy realistic classification here.


### Verbs

Verbs are always given in the infinitive:

    géy-en, to go
    bóy-en, to build
    éss-'n, to eat

The majority of infinitives end in *'n*, as in *éss-'n*, to eat; *shlóf-'n*, to sleep; *bláyb'n*, to remain, except those verbs whose root form ends in *m, n, l, y, ng, nk*.  The infinitives for these end in *en*:

    *m*   ném-en (to take)
    *n*   gán-ven-en (to steal)
    *l*   shméy-kh'l-en (to smile)
    *y*   bóy-en (to build)
    *ng*  zíng-en (to sing)
    *nk*  dánk-en (to thank)


*This category of nouns consists of words taken over wholly from the Hebrew and adheres to the plural-forming method of the Hebrew language.

A regular verb in the present tense is conjugated as follows:

éss-'n, to eat

ikh ess (I eat)                mir éss-'n (we eat)
du est (you eat)               ir est (you (plural) eat)
er est (he eats)               zey éss-'n (they eat)
zi est (she eats)

The past tense in Yiddish is formed by adding *hob* or *host* (singular) or *hób-'n* (plural) as an auxiliary word before the verb, and by adding *ge* as a prefix to the verb and *t* as a suffix. The past participle thus formed remains the same throughout.

zóg-'n, to say

ikh hob ge-zógt (I said)       mir hób-'n ge-zógt (we said)
du host ge-zógt (you said)     ir hot ge-zógt (you (plural) said)
er hot ge-zógt (he said)       zey hób-'n ge-zógt (they said)
zi hot ge-zógt (she said)

Verbs conveying motion use a form of the verb "to be," *zayn*, as the auxiliary word before the past participle, which is formed by adding *ge* to the infinitive.

fór-'n, to ride

ikh bin ge-fór-'n (I rode)     mir záyn-en ge-fór-'n (we rode)
du bist ge-fór-'n (you rode)   ir zayt ge-fór-'n (you (plural) rode)
er iz ge-fór-'n (he rode)      zey záyn-en ge-fór-'n (they rode)
zi iz ge-fór-'n (she rode)

The future tense of Yiddish verbs is formed by adding the various forms of "I will," *ikh vel*, to the infinitive.

shlóf-'n, to sleep

ikh vel shlóf-'n (I will sleep)    mir vél-'n shlóf-'n (we will sleep)
du vest shlóf-'n (you will sleep)  ir vet shlóf-'n (you plural) will sleep)
er vet shlóf-'n (he will sleep)    zey vél-'n shlóf-'n (they will sleep)
zi vet shlóf-'n (she will sleep)

The personal pronouns have already been demonstrated in the conjugations above. The possessive pronouns are:

mayn, my          ún-zer, our
dayn, your        áy-er, (plural)
zayn, his         zéy-er, their
ir, her

Adjectives agree in gender with the nouns they modify adding *e* for feminine, neuter, and plural nouns; *er* for masculine nouns.

**sheyn**, pretty, handsome
**a shéy-ner yíng-l**, handsome lad
**a shéy-ne bild**, a pretty picture

The comparative of the basic adjective undergoes a vowel change in many cases:

| | | |
|---|---|---|
| **sheyn**, pretty | **klug**, wise | **hoykh**, high |
| **shén-er**, prettier | **klúg-er**, wiser | **hékh-er**, higher |

The superlative is formed by adding *st* to the adjective, together with the proper gender.

Adjectives with masculine nouns:

**sheyn, shén-er, shén-ster**
**klug, klúg-er, klúg-ster**
**hoykh, hékh-er, hékh-ster**

Adjectives with feminine nouns:

**shéyn-e, shén-er-e, shén-ste**
**klúg-e, klúg-er-e, klúg-ste**
**hóykh-e, hékh-er-e, hékh-ste**

## Adverbs

The adverbs which have an adjective as root are identical to the adjective:

**hoykh**, high (adjective), or highly (adverb)
**kil**, cool (adjective), or coolly (adverb)
**grob**, coarse (adjective), or coarsely (adverb)

There are the usual adverbs of place, time, and number:

**vu?** (where), **do** (here), **dórt-n** (there), **vu-hín?** (where to?), **a-hér** (to here), **a-hín** (to there), **ven?** (when?), **a-mól** (sometime), **kéyn mol** (never).

It is hoped that the reader has been intrigued rather than dismayed with this smattering of Yiddish grammar and that it will lead to further investigation and study. It should, at least serve to familiarize the reader with the many forms of the basic Yiddish entries of the wordbook and aid in their comprehension.

Do not be overly concerned with the technical details of grammar and pronunciation, but concentrate on understanding the Yiddish heard and spoken in American speech today; become acquainted with its uniqueness, its charm, its wit, and its realism.

## THE CALENDAR

The months of the Jewish year are as follows.

| *Month* | *Usually Falls In* |
|---|---|
| **tísh-rey** | September–early October |
| **khésh-v'n** | October–early November |
| **kís-lev** | late November–December |
| **téy-ves** | January |
| **sh-vát** | late January–February |
| **ó-der** | late February–March |
| [**ó-der** II in a leap year] | [March] |
| **ní-s'n** | late March–April |
| **í-yer** | May |
| **sí-v'n** | late May–June |
| **tá-mez** | July |
| **ov** | late July–August |
| **é-lul** | August–early September |

The Hebrew calendar is a lunar calendar in which a month is $29\frac{1}{2}$ days long. Since a calendar cannot have half days, the Hebrew months are either 29 or 30 days long. A lunar year is 354 days long. In order to equalize the lunar calendar with the solar calendar and to prevent the festivals from occurring out of the season which they serve to commemorate, a system of seven leap years in every 19-year cycle was instituted. In a leap year, an entire month, **ó-der** II, is inserted.

The months of the civil calendar are as follows.

| | |
|---|---|
| January | **yá-nu-ar** |
| February | **féb-ru-ar** |
| March | **marts** |
| April | **a-príl** |
| May | **may** |
| June | **yú-ni** |
| July | **yú-li** |
| August | **óy-gust** |
| September | **sep-tém-ber** |

|          |             |
|----------|-------------|
| October  | ok-tó-ber   |
| November | no-vém-ber  |
| December | de-tsém-ber |

The days of the week are as follows:

|           |                |
|-----------|----------------|
| Sunday    | zún-tik        |
| Monday    | món-tik        |
| Tuesday   | dínst-ik       |
| Wednesday | mít-vokh       |
| Thursday  | dó-ner-shtik   |
| Friday    | fráy-tik       |
| Saturday  | shá-bes        |

The numerical days of each month are designated not by numerals, but by the letters of the Yiddish alphabet, each of which has an assigned numerical value:

| | | | | | | | | |
|---|---|---|---|---|---|---|---|---|
| (א) | alef | 1 | (י״א) | yud-alef | 11 | (מ) | mem | 40 |
| (ב) | beys | 2 | (י״ב) | yud-beys | 12 | (נ) | nun | 50 |
| (ג) | gimel | 3 | (י״ג) | yud-gimel | 13 | (ס) | samekh | 60 |
| (ד) | daled | 4 | (י״ד) | yud-daled | 14 | (ע) | ayin | 70 |
| (ה) | hay | 5 | (ט״ו) | tes-vuv | 15 | (פ) | pey | 80 |
| (ו) | vov | 6 | (ט״ז) | tes-zayin | 16 | (צ) | tsadi | 90 |
| (ז) | zayin | 7 | (י״ז) | yud-zayin | 17 | (ק) | kuf | 100 |
| (ח) | khes | 8 | (י״ח) | yud-khes | 18 | (ר) | reysh | 200 |
| (ט) | tes | 9 | (י״ט) | yud-tes | 19 | (ש) | shin | 300 |
| (י) | yud | 10 | (כ) | khof | 20 | (ת) | tof | 400 |
| | | | (ל) | lamed | 30 | | | |

In writing out the numerals for the years according to the Hebrew calendar, thousands are not expressed, i.e., the year 5737 is written as follows:

| Five thousand | seven hundred | thirty | seven | 5 7 3 7 |
|---------------|---------------|--------|-------|---------|
|               | (tof & shin)  | (lamed) | (zayin) | תשל״ז |
| Not written   | ת ש           | ל      | ז     |         |

To calculate the year on the Yiddish calendar from the secular calendar, add 3760, i.e., 1977 = 1977 + 3760 = 5737

To calculate the secular year from the Jewish year, simply subtract 3760 from the Jewish year.

## CARDINAL NUMBERS

1—eyns
2—tsvey
3—dray
4—fir
5—finf
6—zeks
7—zíb-ń
8—akht
9—nayn
10—tsen
11—elf
12—tsvelf
13—dráy-ts'n
14—fér-ts'n
15—fúf-ts'n
16—zékh-ts'n
17—zíb-e-ts'n
18—ákh-ts'n
19—náyn-ts'n

20—tsván-tsig
21—eyn un tsván-tsig
22—tsvey un tsván-tsig
23—dray un tsván-tsig
24—fir un tsván-tsig
25—finf un tsván-tsig
30—dráy-sig
40—fér-tsig
50—fúf-tsig
60—sékh-tsig
70—zíb-i-tsig
80—ákh-tsig
90—náyn-tsig
100—hún-dert
200—tsvey hún-dert
300—dray hún-dert
1000—tóy-z'nt
2000—tsvey tóy-z'nt
3000—dray tóy-z'nt

## ORDINAL NUMBERS

1st—érsht-er
2nd—tsvéy-ter
3rd—drí-ter
4th—fér-ter
5th—fínf-ter
6th—zéks-ter
7th—zí-bi-ter
8th—ákh-ter
9th—náyn-ter
10th—tsén-ter

L

# A

**a-bí,** so long as

**a-bí ge-zúnt,** so long as you have your health

**a-bí vus,** anything at all, any old thing

**adar,** See **oder**

**a-do-nóy,** (Heb., *adonai*). One of the names of God. Jewish tradition carefully avoids the use of God's name "in vain," or out of liturgical or ritual context. The Bible contains several different names for God which are pronounced *adonoy* regardless of how they are spelled. Except in worship or in the performance of a commandment requiring the recitation of a benediction, the euphemism *ha shem*, the Name, is used. (See **adoshem**)

**a-do-shém,** commonly used substitute for God's name in ordinary discourse or study. The word *ha shem* is the preferred substitute; however, in the course of time it became corrupted to *adoshem*. The most sacred name of God, YHWA, is never uttered, neither in prayer, nor in the recital of a benediction, nor in study.

**a-drés (der),** address (house number and street).

**ad-vo-kát (der),** lawyer

**a-fi-kóy-men (der),** (Aramaic, from the Greek, meaning dessert.) The Passover seder (See **seyder**) is concluded by eating a special piece of matsoh (See **matse**), which has been hidden away at the beginning of the meal. Since the seder cannot be concluded without the *afikoymen*, the custom developed, probably as a device to keep up the interest of children throughout the ritual, for children to "steal" the *afikoymen* during the meal, and to offer it to the head of the house in exchange for a gift at the proper time.

**a-fí-le,** (Heb., *afilu*), even though, even if, even

**a-gú-ne (di),** (Heb., *agunah*), an abandoned wife. According to Jewish law, a wife who has not heard from her husband for a number of years may remarry, providing she has proof beyond a doubt that her husband is dead. While the Bible usually demands the testimony of two witnesses to substantiate a matter, in such cases, the Talmud is more lenient and will accept the word of a single witness. The plight of the *agune* is a difficult one, nevertheless, since even one witness to the death of a husband in a distant place is hard to find. The situation became even more serious for orthodox women after the Holocaust in which countless husbands and wives became separated and neither party ever heard from the other again. Without the word of at least one eyewitness a surviving wife was not able to remarry.

**(a) gut yor,** Happy New Year

1

**a-hér,** here
**a-héym,** homeward, home
**a-hín,** there
**a-hín un k'rik,** back and forth, round trip
**akht,** eight
**ákht-sik,** eighty
**ákht-s'n,** eighteen
**a-khúts,** except for, outside of
**a-klál,** (id.), let's get on with it
**ák-s'l (der),** shoulder
**ák-sh'n (der),** (Heb., *akshan*), stubborn one
**ak-shó-nes (dos),** (Heb., *akshanut*), stubborness
**ak-te-rí-se (di),** actress
**ak-ti-yór (der),** actor
**á-le,** all
**á-lef,** first letter of the Hebrew (and Yiddish) alphabet; in Yiddish it is a vowel
    with two pronunciations, according to the indicated vocalization: אָ, **a** as in
    papa; אַ, **a** as in ball.
**á-lef beys (der),** (Heb., *aleph bet*), alphabet
**aleichem sholom,** See **a-léy-khem shó-l'm**
**á-le-mol,** always
**a-léy-khem shó-l'm,** (Heb., *aleikhem shalom*, lit., unto you, peace).  The appro-
    priate response to the greeting *shol'm aleykhem.*
**a-léyn,** alone
**a-lí-ye (di),** (Heb., *aliyah*, going up).  The honor of being called to pronounce the
    benediction at the reading of the Torah (See **toyre**).  Also, emigration to the
    land of Israel.
**ál-men (der),** (Heb., *alman*), widower
**al-mó-ne (di),** (Heb., *almanah*), widow
**alt,** old
**ál-te moyd (di),** old maid, spinster
**ált-er bókh-er (der),** confirmed bachelor
**alts,** all
**a-mól,** once upon a time
**am-ó-rets (der),** (Heb., *am haaretz*, lit., people of the land), an illiterate or un-
    learned person
**a-mu-zír-'n,** to amuse, to enjoy
**án-denk (der),** memento, memorial
**án-der-e (di),** other(s)
**án-der-er (der),** another, other

**án-dersh**, different, differently
**a-ní-ves (dos)**, (Heb., *anivut*), humility
**ant-dék-'n**, to discover
**án-teyl ném-en**, to participate, to take part
**an-tóysht**, disappointed, dismayed
**ant-shúl-dik-'n**, to excuse, to forgive
**ant-víkl-'t**, developed
**a-pa-rát (der)**, camera
**a-pi-kóy-res (der)**, (Heb., *apikoros*, Epicurus), belief in hedonism; generally, nonbeliever
**a-príl**, April
**ap-teýk-er (der)**, pharmacist
**a-ráyn**, in, into
**a-ráyn-gan-ven-en zikh**, to sneak in
**a-ráyn-ge-fal-'n vi a yóv-'n in sú-ke**, (lit., fell in like a pagan into a *suke*), id., like
 a bull in a china shop.
**a-ráyn-mish-'n**, to butt in, to intrude, to meddle
**a-ráyn-zog-'n**, to tell off, to scold
**ár-be kán-fes (der)**, (Heb., *arbah kanfot*, lit.), four corners, a small rectangle of
 cotton, put on over the head and worn under a man's shirt. On each of the
 four corners of the garment is found a ritually knotted fringe. The Bible
 commands Jews to place such fringes on their garments as tokens of their
 faith. Since occidental garb does not permit the attachment of fringes, this
 small undergarment serves the purpose. Pious Jews will allow the fringes to
 drape over the waist of their trousers so that they will be visible, since the
 commandment requires not only the wearing of such fringes, but that the
 wearer shall "see them." (See **tsitses**.)
**ár-bes (der)**, bean, pea
**ár-bes (di)**, beans, peas
**ár-bet (di)**, work, labor
**ár-bet-er (der)**, worker
**ár-b'l (der)**, sleeve
**ár-em (der)**, arm (anat.)
**a-rest-í-r'n**, to arrest
**a-ri-ber**, over
**a-rit-mé-tik (di)**, arithmetic
**a-ro-mát (der)**, aroma
**a-róp**, off, down
**a-róp fun zín-en**, out of one's mind
**a-róyf**, up, upward

**a-róys,** out, out of

**a-róys géb-'n,** to publish, to distribute, to produce

**aróys várf-'n,** to throw out

**a-rúm,** about, around, approximately

**a-rúm-gey-en leý-dik,** to loaf, to be unemployed, to do nothing

**a-rúm-gey-en on a kop,** to be confused, to be upset

**a-rúm-nem-en,** to embrace, to hold

**a-rún-ter,** down, below

**a-sákh,** many

**a-sé-res-a-dib-res (di),** (Heb., *aseret hadibrot*), Ten Commandments

**a-shí-res (dos),** wealth

**ash-ke-ná-zim (di),** European Jews who follow the traditions which originated in medieval German Judaism. Judaism developed essentially into two main streams after the destruction of Jerusalem in the year 70. One group, the *ashkenazim*, migrated over the centuries to England and to central and eastern Europe and developed their unique customs, practices, ritual, and language (Yiddish) which continue to survive, to a greater or smaller degree, in their descendants. The second group, the *sefardim*, settled in the countries that border the Mediterranean, in Europe and the Middle East. They derived their pattern of Jewish life and their language (Ladino) from the Babylonian, Arabic, and Spanish cultures.

**ash té-ts'l (dos),** ashtray

**(a) táp-ton,** to feel, to paw, to touch

**av,** See **ov**

**a-vá-de,** of course, positively, certainly

**a-vék,** away, gone, gone away

**a-vék-gan-ven-en zikh,** to steal away

**a-vék-shar-'n zikh,** to shuffle off, to die

**a-véy-les (dos),** (Heb., *avelut*), bereavement

**a-véy-re (di),** (Heb., *averah*), sin, waste

**av-róm o-ví-nu,** (Heb., *avraham avinu*), Father Abraham, the first of the three patriarchs of the Jewish people.

**á-yen,** the sixteenth letter of the Hebrew (and Yiddish) alphabet: ע , a vowel pronounced as is the *e* in bed, except in words taken wholly from the Hebrew.

**á-yin hó-re (der),** (Heb., *ayin hara*), evil eye. A widely held superstition has it that bad fortune is brought on by an "evil eye." Many amulets and rituals developed over the centuries for warding off the evil eye. The simplest and most common was to deny the effectiveness of the evil eye by adding the phrase *kayn ayin hore*, after participating in, or reporting some happy event: Our son will graduate tomorrow, *kayn ayin hore!*

**aykh,** to you (plur.)
**áyn-fal (der),** idea, thought, plan
**áyn-lad-'n,** to invite
**áyn-red-'n,** to convince
**áyn-red-'n a kind in boykh,** (lit., to talk a child into one's abdomen), high-pressure salesmanship, a con job. *Er ken dir aynred'n* . . . He can talk you into anything.
**áyn-shten-dik,** decent, proper, law-abiding
**áyn-tsol-'n,** to make a deposit, to make a payment
**az,** when, if
**á-zes pó-nim (der),** arrogant, overbearing, impudent person
**a-zéy-ger,** o'clock
**a-zóy,** so, thus

# B

**ba-dí-ner (der)**, male servant

**ba-díng-ung-en (di)**, conditions, terms

**bád-kh'n (der)**, wedding bard and master of ceremonies. This calling flourished in 18th and 19th century eastern Europe. The *badkh'n* was a poet, entertainer, preacher, organizer, and director of all the prenuptial social and ritual events, as well as of the preliminaries of the wedding ceremony itself. He entertained the guests as they formally presented their gifts to the bride and groom, composing original verses and couplets to match each individual donor, the bride and groom, and members of their families. On the day of the wedding, as the bride and her attendants awaited the ceremony, he would preach an exhortative sermon in verse directed to the bride, dealing with her marital responsibilities. Since the wedding day for bride and groom is likened, in Jewish tradition, to Yom Kippur—a day of atonement and of new beginnings, bride and groom fasted all day. The *badkh'n* also directed the processions to the wedding canopy and led in the merrymaking following the ceremony.

**ba-fál'n**, to attack, to fall upon

**ba-fél (der)**, order, command

**ba-fráy-en**, to liberate

**ba-gán-ven-en**, to embezzle, to rob

**ba-géy-gen-ish (der)**, encounter, meeting

**ba-géy-en zélbst-mord**, to commit suicide

**ba-grís-'n**, to greet

**ba-grób-'n**, to bury, or state of being buried

**ba-hált-'n**, to hide, or state of being hidden

**bak (di)**, cheek (anat.)

**ba-kánt-e (di)**, acquaintance

**ba-kánt-er (der)**, acquaintance

**ba-kén-en zikh**, to become acquainted

**bák-'n**, to bake

**ba-kó-she (di)**, (Heb., *bakashah*), request

**ba-kú-men**, to receive

**bald**, soon

**bal-e-bá-tim (di)**, (Heb., root, *baal habayit*, master of the house), bosses, owners, householders

**bal-e-bá-tish**, (Heb., root, *baal habayit*, master of the house), in an appropriate manner, decently, i.e., as befits the master of the house

**bal-e-bós (der)**, (Heb., root, *baal habayit*, master of the house), boss, owner, householder

**bal-e-gó-le (der)**, (Heb., *baal agalah*), wagon master, wagon driver; also a coarse, ill-mannered person

**ba-léy-dik-'n**, to insult

**bal k'rí-e (der)**, (Heb., *baal keriah*), master reader. One competent in Biblical cantillation who can chant from the Torah scroll (See *toyre*) aloud in the synagogue service according to the ancient Jewish system of musical notation.

**bal me-ló-khe (der)**, (Heb., *baal melakha*), craftsman; expert, competent worker

**bal t'fí-le (der)**, (Heb., *baal tefilah*), master of prayer. One competent to lead a prayer service in the Hebrew according to the prescribed musical prayer modes.

**bal t'shú-ve (der)**, (Heb., *baal teshuvah*), a penitent

**ba-mérk-'n**, to notice

**ba-mérk-ung (di)**, remark

**ban (di)**, train

**ba-nán (di)**, banana

**bán-de (di)**, bunch, gang, group

**bank (di)**, bench, seat, also bank

**bank-ír (der)**, banker

**bar (di)**, pear

**ba-rá-be-v'n**, to plunder, to grossly overcharge

**ba-rá-tung (di)**, conference

**barg (der)**, hill, mountain

**ba-rí men zikh**, to boast

**bar míts-ve (der)**, (Heb., *bar mitsvah*). One competent to perform the Biblical and other commandments required of an adult Jew. A young man who has come into his religious majority. Celebrated on or after the 13th birthday, the event marks the boy's assumption of the religious responsibilities of manhood. He is now expected to obey the commandments (to perform *mitsves*). He may be counted as one of the ten men who constitute a quorum for public prayer; (See **miny'n**) he becomes eligible to be called to bless the Torah (See **toyre**) when it is read aloud in the synagogue. (See **aliye**.)

The *bar mitsve* now becomes accountable for his own actions, earning both the rewards and punishment. For most families this is an occasion for great celebration; however, the act which symbolizes the boy's attainment of religious majority is a simple one: his first *aliye*, the first time he pronounces the benedictions over the Torah. It is also customary for the young man to demonstrate a number of synagogue skills, i.e., to chant the prophetic portion for that Sabbath (See **haftoyre**) or to lead in portions or all of the prayer service.

Since the *aliye* is the critical act for the *bar mitsve*, a boy may become a *bar mitsve* on any occasion when the Torah is read in the synagogue: Sabbath mornings and afternoons, Monday and Thursday mornings, and at festival morning services. The term *bar mitsve* commonly refers to the event itself.

**bar mitzvah,** See **bar mitsve**

**ba-shé-fer (der),** the Creator

**ba-shért,** fated, destined

**ba-shlís-'n,** to decide

**ba-shlós-'n,** decided

**ba-shráyb-'n,** to describe

**ba-shtél-'n,** to order

**ba-shtím-en,** to decide

**ba-shtímt,** definite, decided

**ba-shúld-ig-'n,** to accuse

**bas míts-ve (di),** (Heb., *bat mitzvah*), the feminine equivalent of *bar mitsve*. Although similar in name, the status, history, and in many cases, the ritual which marks a girl's coming of age, is not the exact counterpart of the boy's coming of age. The *bas mitsve* concept is an American development no more than 50 to 60 years old. It originated as an early attempt to give girls some measure of equality with boys in religious life. In most American communities, the *bas mitsve* rituals were synthesized by borrowing some ideas from the *bar mitsve* ritual and from a liberalizing of synagogue tradition, which to this time had never assigned any duty or granted any honors to women. In the early days, the *bas mitsve* was given some liturgical assignment, i.e., to read a prayer or to chant the *kiddush* (See **kidish**). More recently she was given the honor of chanting the prophetic portion (See **haftoyre**). However, she was not called to bless the Torah, or to read from the scroll, she was not counted in the prayer quorum (See **miny'n**) nor was she asked to don prayer shawl (See **talis**) or phylacteries (See **t'filin**). She was not required to attend daily worship services nor to pray privately at home.

With the advent of more contemporary concepts of equality for women, many congregations have rethought their attitudes and have decided, on an individual congregational basis, to look upon a *bas mitsve* as they do upon a *bar mitsve,* and to permit her to participate on an equal basis with the men of the congregation.

The *bas mitsve* rituals are celebrated at Friday evening or Sabbath morning services.

**bas mitzvah, bat mitzvah,** See **bas mitsve**

**ba-támt,** tasty, delicious

**ba-tsól-'n,** to pay

**ba-véyg-ung (di),** movement

**ba-vún-der-'n,** to marvel at, to admire

**ba-vúst,** famous, well known

**bay láyt-'ns,** among decent people, i.e., *bay layt'ns* they would have offered to pay for the damage

**báys-'n,** to bite, to itch

**báy-t'l (der),** purse

**ba-zéts-'n di ká-le,** to enthrone the bride. At orthodox weddings it is traditional for the bride to be seated in a place of honor, prior to the ceremony, surrounded by her girl friends. Men are not permitted to her presence. From here, at the appropriate time, she is led by her parents to the wedding canopy (See **khupe)** where she joins the groom and the ceremony is performed.

**ba-zún-der,** separately, alone

**bé-b'l (dos),** pea, bean, any legume

**be-fráy-en,** to liberate

**be-hált-'n,** to hide, to conceal

**be-héy-me (di),** (Heb., *behemah*), domesticated animal, cattle; also dummy, fool

**bék-er (der),** baker

**bek-er-áy (di),** bakery

**be-kóv-e-dik,** (Heb., root, *bekhavod*), with honor; with proper attention to custom and tradition

**be-kvém,** comfortable

**bénk-'n,** to yearn, to be homesick

**béntsh-'n,** to bless

**béntsh-'n góy-m'l,** blessing recited in gratitude for recovery from a serious illness, or for having been spared from death.

**berd'l (dos),** short beard

**bé-ri-ye (di),** (Heb., *beriyah*), competent, efficient person, commonly used to describe a superior cook, housekeeper

**bés-din (dos),** (Heb., *bet din*), religious court, usually presided over by a rabbi who may invite two or more colleagues or learned laymen to sit with him. In most countries where Jews lived, until well into the late 19th century they did not have access to civil courts; therefore, civil matters between two Jews were adjudicated by a *besdin*, which decided cases according to Jewish law.

**bé-ser,** better

**bes-méd-resh (der),** (Heb., *bet hamidrash*), house of study. An area set aside in the traditional synagogue where Jews would gather regularly, on a daily basis, for sacred study. Groups studying on several levels of knowledge and interest would meet before or after daily services to pursue their chosen area of Jewish study, usually under the leadership of a learned layman.

**bes-óy-lom (der)**, (Heb., *bet olam*, lit., house of the world), cemetery, the consecrated burial place of a Jewish community. Jews may not be buried in any but consecrated earth, except in the most severe emergency.

**bet (di)**, bed

**bét-ge-vant (dos)**, bed linens

**béy-de**, both

**beyn (der)**, bone

**b'-éys**, while, during, as

**beys-a-mík-desh (der)**, (Heb., *bet hamikdash*), the Holy Temple which stood on the Temple Mount in ancient Jerusalem. Only one section of the Temple's western wall remains standing. It has become an especially sacred place for all Jews, symbolizing the ancient sanctity that was the Temple.

**beys ye-sóy-mim (der)**, (Heb., *bet yetomin*), orphanage

**béy-tse (di)**, (Heb., *betsah*), egg

**béy-tsim (di)**, eggs, testicles

**beys**, the second letter of the Hebrew (and Yiddish) alphabet: ב, pronounced as is the letter *b*.

**beyz**, angry, mad

**bi-é-rekh**, (Heb., *b'erakh*), approximately

**bí-kur khóy-lim**, (Heb., *bikur holim*), the commendable and commanded act (See **mitsve**), of visiting the sick; required of all Jews, not restricted to the clergy.

**bild (dos)**, picture

**bíld-ung (di)**, education, culture; used chiefly in reference to secular knowledge

**bí-lik**, cheap, inexpensive, vulgar

**bí-lik vi borsht**, (lit., as cheap as beet soup); bargain, good buy

**bil-ýet (der)**, ticket

**bí-me (di)**, (Heb., *bimah*), place from which worship is conducted in the synagogue; pulpit

**bin**, am (first pers. sing.)

**bí-ne (di)**, stage, platform

**bín-y'n (der)**, (Heb., *binyan*), building

**bí-sl**, little

**bís-lekh-vays**, little by little, slowly

**bist**, are (second pers. sing.)

**bi-tókh-'n (der)**, faith, confidence

**biz**, until

**biz hún-dert un tsv́an-tsik,** (lit., until one hundred and twenty), may you live a
   long life
**bi-zó-y'n (der),** (Heb., *bizayon*), shame, embarrassment
**blat (der),** page, leaf
**blay (der),** lead (mineral)
**bleykh,** pale, ashen, wan
**blik (der),** glance
**blind,** blind
**blín-tse (di),** thin crepe stuffed with cottage cheese or fruit
**blits (der),** lightning
**blíy-en,** to blossom, to bloom
**bló-te (di),** mud, mire
**bloy,** blue
**blóz-'n,** to blow
**blóz-'n fun zikh,** to boast, to act superior, to be impressed with one's importance
**blut (dos),** blood
**b'méy-le,** anyway, nevertheless
**bó-be (di),** grandmother
**bó-be máy-se (di),** old wive's tale, superstition, exaggeration
**bób-kes (di),** cow dung, nothing, zero
**bód-'n zikh,** to bathe (one's self)
**bókh-er (der),** (Heb., *bahur*), young man, bachelor, chap
**bord (di),** beard
**borsht (der),** beet soup
**bór-ves,** barefoot
**bot'l mákh-'n,** to annul, to dissolve (in a legal sense)
**bóy-dem (der),** attic, garret
**bóy-en,** to build
**boykh (der),** abdomen, belly, stomach
**bóykh-vey-tik (der),** bellyache; vexing problem
**boym (der),** tree
**bóy-m'l (der),** cooking oil
**bóy-tshik (der),** young boy
**bóy-tshik-'l (dos),** very young boy
**brékh-'n té-ler,** (lit., to break plates), marks the conclusion of the betrothal
   ritual, conducted sometime prior to the wedding ceremony. A betrothal contract (See **tnóy-im**) is drawn specifying the names of the bride and groom, the
   date and time of the wedding, the gifts to be exchanged, the dowry, the details of the future financial support guaranteed the couple. The contract is

binding and may be dissolved only with the greatest difficulty. Upon the signing of the agreement a plate is broken as a reminder of the destruction of the Temple.

**brém-en (di)**, eyebrows

**bren (der)**, fire; quick-witted, go-getter

**brén-en**, to burn

**bréng-en**, to bring

**bréy-re (di)**, (Heb., *brerah*), alternative, option, choice

**bríl-'n (di)**, spectacles, eyeglasses

**bril-yánt (der)**, diamond, jewel, extraordinarily bright person

**bris (der)**, (Heb., *b'rit*, covenant), circumcision ritual, removal of penis foreskin. Jewish male children are circumcised on their eighth day, marking the eternal covenant between God and the descendants of Abraham. The circumcision must be performed by a ritual circumciser (See **moy'l**), who pronounces the required benedictions and gives the child his Hebrew name. (Girls are named in the synagogue. The father is called to bless the Torah (See **aliye**), after which a prayer in behalf of the child's good health, containing the formula for naming the girl, is recited.)

**briv (der)**, letter (mail)

**brí-ye (di)**, (Heb., *b'riyah*, creature), clever person, efficient homemaker

**brocheh**, See **brokhe**

**bró-khe (di)**, (Heb., *b'rakhah*), benediction, or praise. The formula about which most Jewish liturgy and rituals are constructed. A benediction marks every act of human life for the Jew, symbolizing the sanctity of even the most basic body functions and activities, and, of course, of the more spiritual acts, as well. An observant Jew will pronounce at least 100 blessings each day in the course of eating, performing body functions, and in carrying out a minimum number of ritual commandments.

**brón-f'n (der)**, whiskey, any kind of alcoholic beverage

**brót-'n**, to roast

**bróy-gez**, (Heb., *b'rogez*, in anger), angry; not on speaking terms, feuding

**broyn**, brown

**broyt (dos)**, bread

**brú-der (der)**, brother

**brust (di)**, breast

**b'shó-lem**, (Heb., root, *shalom*), peace; all in one piece

**b'-sú-le (di)**, (Heb., *betulah*), virgin, maiden

**b'-sú-re (di)**, message, tidings

**bú-be-le**, darling, dear, sweetie

**bukh (der)**, book (only for secular books; a sacred book is *seyfer*)

**búl-be (di),** potato
**búl-ke (di),** roll, small loaf of bread
**búl-van (der),** crude or gross person, oaf, bull in a china shop
**bú-ri-kes (di),** beets
**búr-tsh'n,** to grumble, to mutter under one's breath
**b'yá-li (der),** Short form for *byalistoker plets* 7, a flat roll with pizza-like crust, topped with onion bits and poppy seeds named after Byalistok, a small but renowned Jewish city of prewar Poland.

# C

challeh, See khale
chaluts, See kholuts
chanukah, See khanike
chasene, See khasene
chazan, See khaz'n
chazer, See khaz'r
cheder, See kheyder
chochem, See khokhem
chomets, See khomets
chosid, See khosid
chumash, See khumesh
chutspah, See khutspe

# D

**dakht zikh,** seems to me

**dá-let,** the fourth letter of the Hebrew (and Yiddish) alphabet: ‏ד‎ , pronounced as is the letter *d*

**dá-lis (der),** (Heb., *dalut*), poverty

**dá-me (di),** lady

**dank,** thank-you

**dánk-bar,** thankful

**dánk-en,** to thank

**dárf-'n,** to need

**dár-sh'n (der),** (Heb., *darshan*), preacher, orator

**dá-te (di),** date (calendar)

**dáv-ke,** (Heb., *davka*), especially, only, exactly

**dá-ven-en,** to pray, to recite the prescribed prayers, alone or in the midst of a congregation. Used only in connection with recital of the liturgy; not used for impulsive, meditative, personal prayer.

**dáy-ge (di),** (Heb., *daagah*), worry, care, concern

**dayn,** your

**de-ba-tír-'n,** to debate, to argue, to discuss

**dé-malt,** then

**de-mo-krá-ti-ye,** democracy

**der,** the (masculine definite article)

**dé-rekh é-rets (der),** (Heb., *derekh eretz*, lit., the way of the land), respect, proper behavior, normal custom

**der-fár,** therefore

**der-géy-en di yór-'n,** to aggravate, to annoy, to make life miserable, to pester

**der-hár-gen-en,** (Heb. root, *harog*), to kill, to murder, to assassinate

**der-í-ber,** therefore

**der-lóyb-'n,** to allow

**der-shlóg-'n,** depressed

**der-trúnk-'n vér-'n,** to drown

**der-tséyl-en,** to tell

**der-tsíy-en,** to educate, to rear

**der-váks-'n,** grown, adult

**der-váy-le,** in the meantime

**der-véyl-en,** to elect

**de-tsém-ber,** December

**déy-fek (der)**, (Heb., **dofek**), pulse

**di**, the (fem. sing, all plur.)

**dí-bik (der)**, (Heb. root, to cling), ghost, spirit. In Jewish folklore, the spirit of a deceased that invades the body of a living soul. The famous Yiddish play by S. Ansky, *The Dybbuk*, deals with such a situation and with the attempts of a pious community to exorcize the invading spirit.

**dikh**, you

**dil (der)**, floor, ground

**díl-'n a kop**, to confuse, to annoy, to pester

**din**, thin

**din (der)**, (Heb., *din*), law, judgement

**dinst (di)**, maid, servant

**dínst-ik**, Tuesday

**dir**, to you

**dí-re (di)**, (Heb., *dirah*), residence

**dí-re gelt (di)**, rent (money)

**di-ri-gír-'n**, to direct

**do**, here

**dokh**, although

**dók-ter (der)**, doctor

**dól-er (der)**, dollar

**dó-ner-shtik**, Thursday

**dor (der)**, generation

**dó-rem**, south

**dorf (der)**, hamlet, village

**dórt-'n**, there, over there

**dos**, the (sing., neuter)

**dóv-'r ákh-'r (der)**, (Heb., *davar aher*, lit., the other thing), swine; supremely distasteful, vulgar, or unethical person, low character

**dray**, three

**dráy-sik**, thirty

**dráy-ts'n**, thirteen

**drek (dos)**, dung, excrement; anything of poor or distasteful quality

**drém-'l (der)**, catnap, snooze

**dréy-d'l (dos)**, spinning top, used especially in games on khanuke

**dréy-kop (der)**, operator, schemer, conniver

**drík-'n**, to press, to squeeze

**dró-she (di)**, (Heb., *d'rashah*), sermon, speech

**drúk-er (der)**, printer

**drúk-'n**, to print

**du**, you

**dú-khen-en,** (Heb., *dukhan*, pulpit), synagogue rite in which the men who are of the tribe of Moses and Aaron, the *koyhanim*, ascend the pulpit, face the Holy Ark, cover their heads with their prayer shawls, (See **taleysim**) holding their hands aloft and in ancient tune, chant the Priestly Blessing as prescribed in the Bible: "The Lord Bless thee and keep thee . . . "

**durkh,** through

**dúrkh-fal (der),** the failure, the flop

**dúrkh-ku-men,** to agree, to come to terms

**dursht (der),** thirst

**dybbuk,** See **dí-bik**

# E

**éf-sher,** (Heb., *efshar*), may, possibly, perhaps

**ekht,** pure

**ék-l-dik,** disgusting

**ékl-en,** to disgust

**é-lef,** eleven

**e-le-men-tár-shul (di),** elementary school

**él-en-boy-g'n (der),** elbow

**él-'nt,** deserted, alone, lonely

**e-li-yó-u a-nó-vi,** (Heb., *eliyahu hanavi*), Elijah the Prophet

**él-ul,** (Heb., *elul*), twelfth month of the Hebrew calendar; a month of spiritual preparation for the coming high holy days

**é-mes (der),** (Heb., *emet*), truth

**é-mes-e velt (di),** (lit., the true world), world to come

**é-mets-er,** someone

**énd-gilt-ik,** final

**ént-fer (der),** answer, reply, response

**é-pes,** something

**é-p'l (der),** apple

**é-p'l tsí-mes (der),** applesauce

**er,** he

**erd (di),** earth, ground, soil

**é-rev,** (Heb., *erev*), eve of . . .

**é-rev shá-bes,** (Heb., *erev shabbat*), Sabbath eve

**é-rev yón-tef,** (Heb., *erev yom tov*), holiday eve

**ér-lekh,** honest, honorable, reliable

**es,** it

**es!,** eat!

**es brent!,** fire!, afire

**es hot mayn bó-bes tam,** (lit., it has my grandmothers' taste), it tastes bad, something of poor quality

**é-sig (der),** vinegar

**es makht nit oys,** it doesn't matter

**és-'n,** to eat

**és-'n (dos),** food, nourishment

**és-rig (der),** (Heb., *etrog*), citron. One of the four symbols used on the Feast of Booths (See **sukes**) in combination with a palm branch (See **lulev**), a willow twig (Heb., *aravah*), and a myrtle branch (Heb., *hadas*). All four are grasped together in both hands and waved to the four corners of the earth, to the heavens and down to the earth symbolizing God's providence and sovereignty.

**es shteyt mir nit on,** it is beneath me

**es tut zikh op khóy-shekh,** chaos, things are in a mess, riot in progress

**ét-li-khe,** several

**ey (dos),** egg

**éy-bersht-e fun shtéy-s'l (dos),** (lit., the substance that arises to the top of the mortar); cream of the crop

**éy-bik,** eternally

**éy-bi-kayt (di),** eternity

**eyd (der),** (Heb., *ed*), witness

**éy-dem (der),** son-in-law

**éy-der,** before, ere

**éy-d'l,** courteous, gentle, noble

**éy-fe-le (dos),** infant

**éy-fer-zukht (di),** jealousy

**ey-g'n-tí-mer (der),** owner, proprietor

**eyl mó-ley . . . ,** (Heb., *el maleh* . . . ), Lord full of . . . the opening words, and the title, of the memorial prayer for the eternal peace of the dead. Recited at funerals, memorial services, dedication of gravestones, etc.

**éy-nik-'l (dos),** grandchild

**eyns,** one

**éyn-tsik-er (der),** single, only

**éy-tse (di),** (Heb., *etzah*), advice, idea

**éy-z'l (der),** donkey, ass

# F

**fa-brík (di),** factory
**fakh (der),** trade, craft
**fál-en,** to fall
**fa-rán,** to exist, exists
**farb (di),** color
**far-báy-t'n di yóyts-res,** to get things fouled up; *yoytsres* (Heb., *yotzrot*) are special prayers added to the liturgy on the festivals, each festival having its own unique additions applicable only to that festival. To recite the *yoytsres* for *peysakh* on *sukes* would foul things up, indeed.
**far-bét-'n,** to invite
**far-bís-'n-er (der),** (lit., one with clenched lips), one with a sour, angry forbidding facial expression
**far-bít-ert,** embittered
**far-blón-zhen,** to lose one's way
**far-bréng-en,** to pass the time, to have a good time
**far der tsayt,** before one's time, early
**far-dín-en,** to earn
**far-dín-er (der),** breadwinner, wage earner
**far-dórb-'n,** depraved, rotten
**far-drís-'n,** to chafe, to be annoyed, to be hurt, to be sorry
**far-fál-en,** lost opportunity, too late, too bad
**far-fál-en ge-vór-'n,** to have become lost, to have disappeared
**far-féyl-en,** to neglect, to overlook a duty or responsibility
**far-fír-'n,** to seduce, to mislead
**fár-f'l (di),** noodle flakes
**far-fór'n,** to arrive; to get to the wrong place
**far-fóylt,** rotten, moldy (food or vegetation)
**far-gáng-en-hayt (di),** past
**far-gés-'n,** to forget
**far-géyn,** to fade, to set (as in sunset)
**far-gín-en,** to be pleased at another's good fortune
**far-gláykh-'n,** to compare
**far-gváld-ik-'n,** to rape
**far-kí-lung (di),** cold
**far-kírts-'n,** to shorten
**far-knást,** engaged, betrothed

20

**far-krénk-'n**, to use up one's money to cure an illness
**far-krímt-er (der)**, sour-faced
**far-mákh-'n**, to close
**far-méyg-'n (der)**, fortune, assets
**far-mísh-'n**, to stir up, to mix up (as in cooking: to mix up a batter), to cook up a deal
**far-móg-'n**, to own
**far-nákht**, early evening, sunset
**far-nú-men**, busy, occupied
**far-sám-en**, to poison
**far-shém-en**, to embarrass, to shame, to humiliate
**far-shlép-te krenk**, a long illness; a long story, a drawn-out affair
**far-shpét-ik-'n**, to be late, tardy
**far-shtér-'n**, to spoil, to cast a pall over, to thwart
**far-shtéy-en**, to understand
**far-shvínd-'n**, to disappear
**fár-takh (der)**, apron
**far tóg**, before daylight; daybreak
**far-tshád-et**, groggy, incoherent
**far-váyl-ung (di)**, amusement, entertainment
**far vús**, why
**far-zá-men**, to be late, to miss out
**far-zám-lung (di)**, gathering
**fást-'n**, to fast
**fáy-er (der)**, fire
**fáyf-'n**, to whistle, to boo
**fayn**, decent, good quality
**fáyn-kukh-'n (der)**, omelet
**faynt (der)**, enemy
**faynt hób-'n**, to hate
**fe!**, phew!, terrible!, ugh!
**féb-ru-ar**, February
**fé-fer (der)**, pepper (spice and vegetable)
**fénd-'l (dos)**, saucepan
**fén-ster (der)**, window
**ferd (der)**, horse; also fool, sap
**férsh-ke (di)**, peach
**fér-tsik**, forty
**fér-ts'n**, fourteen

**fés-'l (dos)**, barrel

**fet**, fat

**fé-ter**, uncle

**fey**, the weaker version of the seventeenth letter of the Hebrew (and Yiddish) alphabet: פ, pronounced as is the letter *f*. When it occurs at the end of a word it is printed ף.

**féy-ge-le (dos)**, little bird; also male homosexual

**féy-ik**, talented, competent

**féy-l'n**, to need, to be short of, missing

**fíd-l (der)**, violin

**fi-lo-só-fi-ye (di)**, philosophy

**finf**, five

**fín-ger (der, di)**, finger (sing. and plu.)

**fín-ger-hut (der)**, thimble

**fínkl-en**, to sparkle, to twinkle

**fín-ster**, dark

**fir**, four

**fir ká-shes (di)**, the "Four Questions" asked by the youngest child at the *pey-sakh seyder* (See **ma nishtane**)

**fír-me (di)**, company, firm

**fír-'n**, to lead

**fír-'n far der noz**, to lead by the nose

**fír-'n in bod a-ráyn**, (lit., to lead one to the bathhouse), to pull the wool over one's eyes

**fish (der)**, fish

**fí-s'l (dos)**, small foot; also furniture leg

**fitsh nas**, wringing wet

**fleysh (dos)**, meat, flesh

**fléysh-ik**, food containing meat or meat by-products (mostly in connection with dietary laws), See **kashres**.

**fléysh-mark (der)**, meat market

**fleyt (di)**, flute

**flig (di)**, fly

**flíg-'l (der)**, wing

**flíy-en**, to fly

**floym (di)**, plum, prune

**fó-dem (der)**, thread

**fó-der-'n**, to demand

**folg mir a gang!**, I'm not about to do that, I couldn't care less, no way, fat chance!

**folk (dos)**, people, nation, folk
**fón-fer (der)**, (lit., one who speaks nasally or indistinctly), faker, one who sits on both sides of the fence, one who makes excuses, procrastinator
**fór-leyg-'n**, to suggest
**fórsh-er (der)**, scientist, researcher
**fórsh-'n**, to investigate
**fór-shtel-ung (di)**, performance
**fó-t'r (der)**, father
**fóy-g'l (der)**, bird
**foyl**, lazy, rotten (food)
**frá-ge (di)**, question
**frask (der)**, slap
**fray**, free
**frayn-dí-ne (di)**, friend (fem.)
**fraynt (der)**, friend (masc.)
**fráynt-lakh**, friendly
**fráynt-shaft (di)**, friendship
**fráy-tik**, Friday
**freg mikh b'khéy-rem**, (id.) don't ask me, I have no idea
**frég-'n**, to ask
**frémd-er (der)**, outsider, stranger, alien
**frés-er (der)**, glutton
**frés-'n**, to overeat, to eat (for animals), to eat in a gross, vulgar manner
**freyd (di)**, joy, happiness
**fréy-lakh**, happy, festive
**fri**, early
**fri (der)**, morning
**fríd-'n**, peace
**frí-ling (der)**, spring
**frír-'n**, to freeze
**frish**, fresh
**frish, ge-zúnt un me-shú-ge**, (lit., fresh, healthy, and crazy), You must be out of your mind!
**froy (di)**, woman
**frum**, pious, devout
**fúf-tsik**, fifty
**fúf-ts'n**, fifteen
**ful**, full
**ful-kóm**, complete, grown, adult
**fun**, from
**fus (der)**, foot, leg

# G

gá-be (der), (Heb., *gabbai*), synagogue elder

gá-bi-te (di), wife of synagogue elder; woman active in communal affairs

gal (di), gallbladder

gan eden, See gan eyd'n

gá-nev (der), (Heb., *ganav*), thief

gan éyd-'n, (Heb., *gan eden*), Garden of Eden, paradise

ga-néy-ve (di), (Heb., *ganevah*), robbery

gá-nik (der), porch, terrace

gants, whole, complete

gán-ven-en, to steal

ganz (di), goose

gart'l (dos), belt, sash

gas (di), street

gast (der), guest

gást-fraynd-likh-kayt (dos), hospitality

gát-kes (di), underwear

gáy-ve (di), (Heb., *gaavah*), arrogance, conceit

gaz (di), gas (the vapor)

gáz-l'n (der), (Heb., *gazlan*), robber, thief, highwayman, crook

ge-béks (dos), pastry

geb'n, to give

ge-bót (dos), law, commandment

ge-bóy-r'n, born

ge-brót-'ns (dos), roast

ge-dénk-'n, to remember

ge-díkht, thick, dense, heavy

ge-dóyr-'n, to last, to take (in time)

ge-dúld (di), patience

ge-énd-ikt, finished, over

ge-fál-en-er (der), fallen one, one in reduced circumstances

ge-fár (der), danger

ge-fél-'n, to please, to find favor

ge-fér-lakh, dangerous

ge-fíl (dos), emotion, feeling, sensitivity

ge-fíl-te fish (di), boiled fish patties, usually of carp or whitefish. (Lit., filled
    fish, because it was customary to wrap the patties in fish skin before cooking,

so they appeared to be "stuffed" or "filled.") A favorite first course for the Sabbath eve meal.

**ge-fín-en,** to find

**ge-hé-nem (der),** (Heb., *gehinom*), refers to the Valley of Gehinom, located immediately south of the ancient city of Jerusalem, where pagan rites involving the sacrifice of young children were once conducted. There is no special word in Jewish tradition for what the western world calls "hell." For Jews, this valley, with all its brutal and loathesome associations, gradually came to mean purgatory.

**ge-hér-'n,** to belong to

**ge-hók-te tsó-res,** (lit., chopped troubles), in a bad way, doing poorly, beset by misfortune.

**gel,** yellow

**ge-lég-'n-hayt (di),** opportunity, chance, occasion

**ge-lég-er (dos),** place to sleep, bed

**ge-líng-en,** to succeed

**gelt (dos),** money

**ge-méyn,** common, low, vulgar

**ge-mó-re (di),** (Heb., *gemarah*, completion), classic commentary on the code of Jewish law, the *mishnah*. Written in Aramaic in the period between the third and fifth century of the Common Era by successive generations of scholars known as *amoraim* (interpreters). The *mishnah* had been completed earlier, in the year 200, by scholars known as *tanaim* (teachers). Together, the *mishnah* and the *gemarah* constitute the two major sections of the *talmud*. (See **mishne, talmud.**)

**ge-núg,** enough

**ge-pókt un ge-móz-'lt,** (lit., one who has had the pox and the measles), experienced, learned the hard way, knows the ropes

**ge-rékht,** right, correct

**ge-rékht-i-kayt (di),** justice

**ge-ríkht (dos),** court, judgement

**ge-rírt,** mentally unbalanced

**ge-rót-'n,** to be successful

**ge-rót-'n in . . . ,** to resemble, to take after

**ge-rúkh (der),** fragrance, odor, smell

**ge-shéft (dos),** business

**ge-shéyn,** to occur

**ge-shíkh-te (di),** history, story

**ge-shlékht (dos),** sex

**ge-shlós-'n,** closed

**ge-shmák**, taste, tasty, delicious, tasteful
**ge-shréy (dos)**, outcry, scream
**gest (di)**, company (social)
**get (der)**, (Heb., *get*), divorce
**ge-tráy**, loyal, faithful
**ge-ú-le (di)**, (Heb., *geulah*), redemption
**ge-váld!**, help! (when preceded by *"mit,"* *mit gevald*, connotes something accomplished with force or violence, under duress)
**ge-váld-e-v'n**, to cry out, to protest loudly
**ge-vént**, depends on
**ge-vér (dos)**, firearm
**ge-véyn (dos)**, weeping
**ge-véynt-lekh**, ordinarily, usually
**ge-vóyn-hayt (di)**, habit
**ge-vú-re (di)**, (Heb., *gevurah*), strength, heroism, courage
**géy-en**, to go
**gey in d'r-érd a-ráyn**, go to hell
**géy-le (di)**, (lit., yellow ones), in the early 20th century, this term referred to the more integrated immigrants, those who had been here for a longer time. New immigrants were called *grine*, greenhorns.
**géy-nets (der)**, yawn
**géy-'n oyf ré-der-'n**, (lit., to go on wheels), great activity, much rushing about, bedlam, chaos
**gey shray khay ve-ká-yom**, (lit., go, cry out: the living, eternal God), helpless, a crying in the wilderness, talk to the wall, complain to God
**ge-záng (dos)**, song, singing
**ge-zéts (dos)**, law, statute (secular)
**ge-zéy-le (di)**, theft
**ge-zúnt (dos)**, health, well-being
**gím-el**, third letter of the Hebrew (and Yiddish) alphabet: ג , pronounced as is the letter *g*.
**gír-'n (di)**, brains, (anat.)
**glat**, smooth
**glat a-zóy**, just because . . .
**glat kó-sh'r**, (Heb., root, *kasher*, clean), meat that meets the strictest requirements of the dietary laws. The ritual slaughterer (See **shoykhet**) is required to examine the lungs of a slaughtered animal to check on the health of the animal. If the lungs are marked by tuberculosis nodules the animal is declared unkosher (See **treyf**). If there is evidence of healed tuberculosis nodules, indicating that the animal had recovered from the disease, the meat is

declared to be kosher. When the lungs show neither recovery scars nor disease nodules, and is smooth (See **glat**), the animal is declared *glat* (smooth) *kosh'r*. The term today is broadly used to indicate scrupulously inspected and prepared meat. The ultra-orthodox and many hasidic sects will eat only *glat kosh'r* meat.

**glaykh,** straight, direct

**gláykh-'n,** to like, to admire

**glet (der),** caress

**glet'n,** to caress, to pet, to soothe

**glid (der),** organ (anat.)

**glik (dos),** luck, good fortune, happiness

**glík-lakh,** lucky, happy

**glitsh (der),** slip, skid

**glítsh-'n,** slip, skid, ice-skate, slide

**glóy-b'n (dos),** faith, religious principles, belief

**glóy-b'n,** believe

**gloz (di),** glass, tumbler

**g'néy-vish,** sneaky, fraudulent, tricky

**gold (dos),** gold

**góld-i-ne me-dí-ne (di),** (Heb., *medinah*, country), the Golden Land, what East European immigrants called America

**gó-les (der),** (Heb., *galut*), diaspora, any community outside of the Holy Land

**gonif,** See **ganev**

**góp-'l (der),** fork

**gor,** very

**gór-g'l (der),** throat, gullet

**gór-nisht,** nothing, nothing at all

**gór-nisht mit gór-nisht,** worthless, useless

**górt-'n (der),** garden

**got,** God

**got di ne-shó-me shúld-ik,** (lit., one who is in debt to God for his soul), the acme of innocence; butter wouldn't melt in his mouth; one who pretends to be innocent

**gót-e-nyu,** dear God, loving Father

**got tsu dánk-en,** Thank God

**got zol óp-hit-'n!,** God forbid!

**goy (der),** gentile (masc.)

**góy-e (di),** gentile (fem.)

**góy-lem (der),** (Heb., *golem*, dummy), simpleton, fool, moron. A famous legend tells the story of Rabbi Loew of Prague of the 16th century, who fashioned an automaton (*goylem*) into which he was able to instill life by placing in his mouth a slip of paper containing the secret, mystical name of God. The rabbi hoped that the *goylem* would help protect the long persecuted Jewish community. While the plan worked for a while, the *goylem*, as he grew more human, became less tractable and the rabbi was finally forced to destroy him.

**góy-resh (der)**, divorced man

**góy-r'l (der)**, fate, destiny

**grág-er (der)**, noisemaker used to drown out the name of Haman when it is read from the Scroll of Esther on Purim.

**gregger**, See **grager**

**gré-nets (der)**, border, boundary

**grepts (der)**, belch

**greyt**, ready

**grin**, green

**grín-er (der)**, (lit., green one); new immigrants of the early 20th century eastern European immigration period. (See **geyle**.)

**gring**, easy

**grins (dos)**, vegetable, salad

**grí-vi-nes (di)**, crisp bits of the skin of fowl which remain after the fat has been rendered, cracklings

**grízh-'n**, to grumble, to gripe, to needle

**grob**, coarse, vulgar, fat

**gró-'n**, to dig, to excavate

**gró-'r yung (der)**, coarse fellow, boor

**groys**, large

**groz (dos)**, grass

**g'rú-she (di)**, divorcee

**gut**, good

**gút-e nakht**, good night

**gút-er brí-der**, (lit., good brother); buddy, pal, friend

**gut ge-zógt**, (lit., well said), here, here!, you certainly told him off

**gut mór-gen**, good morning

**gút-'n óv-'nt**, good evening

**gút-'n tog**, good day, good-bye

**g'vir**, rich man.

# H

**hagadah,** See **hagode**

**ha-gó-de (di),** (Heb., *hagadah*, lit., the telling). The *hagode* is the liturgical text and ritual manual used at the Passover *seyder*. It recounts the history of the Jewish people from the time of Abraham, through the liberation of his descendants from Egyptian bondage, through the use of songs, stories, parables, Talmudic excerpts, questions, and answers. It also contains the instructions and benedictions for the 13 ritual acts of the *seyder*.

**hak (di),** axe, a sharp blow

**hakh-nó-se (di),** income

**hak-mé-ser (der),** cleaver, kitchen chopping tool

**hak'n,** to chop

**hák-'n a tsháy-nik,** (lit., to bang a teakettle); to drone on, to bend one's ear, to bore to death

**halb,** half

**haldz (der),** throat

**háldz-'n,** embrace

**halle,** See **kha-le**

**ha-le-váy,** (Heb., *hal'vay*), hopefully, would that

**ha-ló-khe (di),** (Heb., *halakha*, the going), entire spectrum of Jewish law

**hált-'n,** keep, hold

**hált-'n dos moyl,** [lit., to keep one's mouth (closed)] ; to keep silent

**hált-'n shmol,** the situation is critical

**hált-'n zikh bay di záyt-'n,** (lit., to hold one's sides); to die laughing; to split one's sides with laughter

**halutz,** See **khaluts**

**há-mer (der),** hammer

**hánd-'l (der),** business, commerce

**hánd'l-en,** to deal, to do business, to bargain

**ha-nó-e hób-'n,** (Heb., *hanaah*, pleasure), to take pleasure from

**hant (di),** hand

**hanukkah,** See **khanuke**

**harts (dos),** heart

**has (der),** hatred

**ha-shem,** [Heb., *ha shem*, the Name (of God)]. A substitute name for God used by Jews when they are not engaged in prayer, or in the observance of a commandment requiring the recitation of a benediction. (See **brokhe, adoshem.**)

**hasid,** See **khosid**

**hasidim,** See **khosid, kh'sidim**

**has-kó-le (di),** the Jewish Enlightenment movement which flourished in central and eastern Europe during the 19th century. It proposed that Jews broaden their interest and participation in the secular world and in the enlargement of the scope of Jewish education to include all aspects of world science, culture, and philosophy. Jews would then be competent to take their rightful place among their European neighbors, once the emancipation from the strictures of the ghetto was achieved. It was the sincere belief of the leaders of the *haskole* that the first blossoming of that emancipation was already in progress in their time. They also held that one important factor which stood in the way of the complete emancipation of Jews was the exclusively religious education which Jewish children were receiving at that time. They made a great effort to enlarge the school curricula to include a wide range of secular subjects.

**havdalah,** See **havdole**

**hav-dó-le,** (Heb., *havdalah*, separation), the ritual which marks the conclusion of the Sabbath. A number of benedictions and hymns are chanted in the ceremony, in which a multiwick braided candle, a spice box, and a cup of wine are used. The ceremony symbolizes the sadness of the Jew over the departure of the Sabbath and articulates his hopes for the week to come. *havdole* may not be recited until three stars can be seen in the evening sky.

**haynt,** today, nowadays

**háyz-'l (dos),** (lit., little house), brothel

**hazzan,** See **khaz'n**

**he-bréy-ish,** Hebrew (language)

**heder,** See **kheyder**

**héf-ker,** (Heb., *hefker*), open, unregulated, wide-open, lawless, undisciplined

**héf-ker pét-rish-ke,** (lit., undisciplined parsley) anything goes

**hék-dish (der),** poorhouse

**held (der),** hero

**hélf-'n,** to help

**hélf-'n vi a tóyt-'n bán-kes,** (lit., as effective as cupping a corpse), wasted effort, useless to try. Cupping (*shetl'n bankes*) was an old remedy for chest or back pains, colds, and inflammations. A dozen or so small round-bottom glass cups were applied to the affected area by means of vacuum suction. The air was evacuated from the cups by swabbing the inside with alcohol and then igniting it. When the flame died, the cup was quickly placed on the skin. The suction caused the blood near the surface of the skin to be drawn there much in the same fashion as some liniments accomplish this in our day.

**helft,** half

**hemd (dos),** shirt
**herbst (der),** autumn, harvest time
**hér-'n,** to hear
**heshvan,** See **kheshv'n**
**hés-ped (der),** (Heb., *hesped*), eulogy
**hey,** the fifth letter of the Hebrew (and Yiddish) alphabet; ה, pronounced as is
   the letter *h*.
**héy-lik,** holy
**héyl-'n,** to heal, to cure
**héy-mish,** homey, familiar
**heys,** hot
**héys'n,** named, called, to order, to command
**héyz-rik,** hoarse
**hík-en,** to stutter
**hilf (di),** help, assistance
**hím-'l (der),** heaven, sky
**hínk-en,** to limp
**hínt-'n (der),** behind, buttocks
**his-lá-ves (der),** (Heb., *hitlaavut*), religious ecstasy
**hít-'n,** to guard
**hits (di),** heat, fever
**hit zikh!,** take care, look out
**hób-'n,** to have
**hób-'n a déy-e,** to have a say, to be in a position to determine a course or policy
**hób-'n a pó-nim,** to appear as, to look like
**hób-'n tsu zíng-'n un tsu zóg-'n,** (lit., to have something to sing, something to
   say); to have endless bother or trouble, to have many complications arise
**hóf-'n,** to hope
**hó-lib-tses (di),** stuffed cabbage
**holts (dos),** wood, lumber
**hó-men-tash (der),** pastry made in celebration of Purim.  Triangular sweet buns
   filled with poppy seeds or prune jam.  They get their name (Haman' pockets)
   from the villain of the Scroll of Esther.
**homets,** See **khomets**
**hon (der),** rooster
**hón-ik (der),** honey
**hor (der),** hair
**hóts-ke (di),** bump, song and dance routine
**hóyf (der),** courtyard, court (of a king or of a hasidic rabbi)
**hoykh,** tall; loud

**hoyt (di),** skin
**hoyz (di),** house, home
**hóy-z'n (di),** trousers
**hu-há (der),** fuss, excitement
**humash,** See **khumesh**
**hún-dert,** hundred
**hún-ger (der),** hunger
**hún-ge-rik,** hungry
**hunt (der),** dog
**hu-re-ráy (di),** fornication
**hust (der),** cough
**hutspah,** See **khutspe**

# I

í-ber-al, everywhere
í-ber-bay-s'n (dos), breakfast
í-ber-bayt-'n, to exchange
í-ber-bet-'n, to reconcile, to make up, to ask for forgiveness
í-ber-ik, over, excess
í-ber-ker-i-nish (dos), turmoil
í-ber-khaz-er-'n, to rehearse, to repeat
í-ber-kuk-'n, to look over, to review
í-ber-rays-'n, to break off, to interrupt
í-ber-shrek-'n, to frighten, to terrorize
í-ber-trakht-'n, to speculate, to worry
í-ber-trayb-'n, to exaggerate
í-ber-zets-'n, to translate
í-ber-zéts-ung (di), translation
í-ker (der), (Heb., *ikar*), root, principle, crux
ikh, I
im, to him
im yír-tse ha-shém, (Heb., *im yirtze ha shem*), God willing
in der fremd, to be among strangers, outsider
in-der-frí, morning
in d'rerd a-ráyn, go to hell, to hell with it
in-ér-gets nit, nowhere
ín-e-vey-nik, within, inside
in éy-nem, together
in gánts-'n, entirely, completely
in kas, (Heb., *kaas*, anger), angry
ir, to her; you (plur.)
itst, now
iyar, See iyer
í-yer, (Heb., *iyar*), eighth month of the Hebrew calendar. Israel's Independence
    Day, *yom haatzmaut*, is celebrated on the fifth day; *lag ba-omer*, known as
    the Scholar's Holiday falls on the 18th.
iz, is (he, she)

# K

**ka-bó-les pó-nim (der)**, (Heb., *kabbalat panim*), reception

**káb-ts'n (der)**, pauper

**ká-dish (der)**, (Heb., *kaddish*, sanctification). A doxology recited in praise of God at formal worship services. There are several types of *kadish*, recited on different occasions. Most Jews who speak of reciting *kadish* are referring to the Mourner's Kaddish (Heb., *kadish yatom*). The language of the *kadish* is Aramaic, the language of home and street of Jews in the centuries following the Babylonian captivity, app. 5th century before the Common Era. Hebrew was reserved only for prayer and sacred study. *kadish* was originally recited by students and teachers at the conclusion of a session of sacred study. Gradually, it was brought into the developing liturgy of the early synagogue to mark the conclusion of specific sections of the service. It then became associated with the conclusion of the life of a parent. It became traditional for a son to recite the *kadish* at the termination of a parent's life and for the ensuing year of mourning. The *kadish* contains no reference to death or to parents, but speaks of the continuing faith of the living in God and in His plan for human life. It is especially meaningful for the mourner to profess his faith in the face of the deep loss he has suffered. In our time, children recite *kadish* for parents for the 11 months following the death and on each anniversary of the death (See **yortseit**) that follows. Likewise, parents for children. Siblings, mates, etc. are required to recite *kadish* for the first 30 days following the funeral.

**ka-dó-khes (dos)**, (Heb., *kadahat*, lit., shaking with the heat and with the cold), ague, convulsions

**ká-le (di)**, (Heb., *kallah*), bride

**ka-lósh-'n (di)**, galoshes, overshoes

**kál-ye mákh-'n**, spoil, hinder, disrupt, put out of order

**kál-yi-ke (der)**, cripple, inept one, poor craftsman

**kalt**, cold

**ka-méy-e (di)**, amulet, charm against the evil eye

**kám-ts'n (der)**, (Heb., *kamtzan*), miser, penny pincher

**kán-tshik (der)**, cat-o-nine tails

**ká-pel-yush (der)**, derby

**ka-pó-re (di)**, (Heb., *kaparah*), atonement, forgiveness; i.e., *a kapore far di zind*, an atonement for sin; sacrificial fowl used in an ancient ritual on the day before Yom Kippur (See **yom kiper**). Called *shlog'n kapores*, the ritual consists in circling the head of the penitent three times so that his sins may be symbolically transferred to the fowl. The formula, "This fowl is a sacrifice in my stead," is repeated three times. The bird is then slaughtered according to tradition (See **shoykhet**) and given to the poor. The custom had its roots in the Biblical practice of slaughtering a scapegoat animal to atone for the sins of an individual or group.

**ka-pó-te (di)**, long coat worn by religious Jews

**ka-príz (der)**, whim, caprice

**karg**, stingy; not quite enough, lacking

**kárg-er (der)**, miser

**karsh (di)**, cherry

**kar-tó-f'l (di)**, potato

**kas (der)**, (Heb., *kaas*), anger

**ká-she (di)**, buckwheat groats, a common east European cereal. Another meaning is the one which is derived from the Hebrew word, *kushiyah*, question. The play on words permits the evolution of such expressions as, *farkokh'n a kashe*, which could mean to cook up a batch of groats, or, more idiomatically, to cook up a mess of trouble or complications. The "Four Questions" asked by the youngest child at the *seyder* are called, *di fir kashes*.

**kásh-res (dos)**, (Heb., *kashrut*), the entire regimen of the dietary laws. Briefly, animal food: only fish that have both fins and scales; animals that part the hoof and chew the cud. Animals must be ritually slaughtered (See **shoykhet**). Forbidden are shellfish, worms, snails, flesh torn from a living animal. Mixing milk and meat, or their derivatives is forbidden. A period of time (one to six hours, according to local custom) must pass in order to eat meat after having eaten dairy food. Fish are neither meat nor dairy (See **pareve**).

**kashruth**, See **kashres**

**kást-'n (der)**, box, crate, coffin, chest

**kats (di)**, cat

**kátsh-ke (di)**, duck

**ka-val-yér (der)**, lover, boyfriend, suitor, man-about-town

**ká-ve (di)**, coffee

**ká-ve-ne (di)**, watermelon

**káy-en**, to chew

**káy-lekh-dik**, round

**kayn**, not any, no, none

**kayn áy-en hó-re**, (Heb., *b'li ayin hara*, lit., spare us the evil eye) id., knock on wood

**k'day**, advisable, worthwhile

**k'dey**, (Heb., *k'dei*), in order that, so that

**ké-g'n**, against, versus

**ke-híl-e (di)**, (Heb., *kehillah*), community, congregation
**kékh-er (der)**, chef, cook (masc.)
**kékh-ne (di)**, cook (fem.)
**ké-ler (der)**, cellar
**kelt (di)**, cold, frost
**kémf-'n**, to struggle, to wage war
**kém-'l (dos)**, comb
**kén-en**, to know, to be able, to know how, to be skilled in
**kér-per (der)**, body
**ké-she-ne (di)**, pocket
**kest (di)**, room and board, full support
**kéy-le (der)**, (Heb., *kli*), vessel, dish
**kéy-lim (di)**, dishes
**kéyn-er**, no one
**keyt (di)**, chain
**kez (der)**, cheese
**kha-bár (der)**, bribe, bribery
**khad-gád-ye (der)**, (Aramaic, *had gadya*, one little kid), favorite Passover *seyder* song concerning a baby goat which Father brought for two *zuzim.* Idiomatically: jail, hoosegow
**kha-lát (der)**, robe
**khá-le (di)**, (Heb., *hallah*), Sabbath loaf. In the Bible it refers to the priest's share of baking dough. It is the braided, white egg-loaf of bread eaten on the Sabbath and festivals, although there is no prohibition against its use on ordinary weekdays. On *rosh hashanah* (See **rosheshone**) the shape of the *khale* is round, symbolizing the hope for the continuity of life. In memory of the ancient ritual in the Holy Temple, and in compliance with Biblical command, pious women cast a piece of dough into the fire, when preparing *khale.*
**khá-lesh-'n**, (Heb., *halash*, weak), to faint
**kha-lósh-es**, terrible, something bad enough to induce a fainting spell; i.e., *di forshtelung iz khaloshes*, this performance is awful.
**kha-ní-fe (di)**, (Heb., *hanifah*), flattery
**khá-ni-ke**, (Heb., *hanukkah*), Feast of Lights, celebrated for eight days beginning with the 25th of *kislev* on the Hebrew calendar. It commemorates the victory of the Jewish resistance under Judah Maccabee over the pagan Syrian forces which sought to enslave Israel, physically and spiritually, in 186 before the Common Era. The Israelites defeated their Syrian oppressors, cleansed the ravaged Temple, and reconstituted a Jewish government. When the Temple had been cleansed and restored to its former sanctity it was ready to be rededicated to the service of God. However, only one small cruze of oil

was found for the Temple Menorah, sufficient only for one day. Miraculously, the oil continued to burn for eight days. Therefore, the festival which celebrates the victory of religious freedom over tyranny came to be observed for eight days. An eight branched *hanukkiah* (*khanike menoyre*) is used. Each night one additional candle is kindled, until finally all eight candles are lit on the eighth night. *khanike* is essentially a home, family-oriented holiday, although there are a number of liturgical additions to the synagogue service. It is a time when families gather, kindle the lights, chant the benedictions, and sing the hymns, then exchange small gifts. The traditional food is the *latke*, potato pancake. Some say, because they are fried in oil they remind one of the miracle of the oil. Because the holiday falls in early winter and includes celebrations with lights and gifts one might be led to believe that *khanike* is the "Jewish Christmas." This is not so. Christmas celebrates the birth of Jesus and of the Christian faith; it is a major festival of the Christian religious calendar. *khanike* is a minor festival, recording one of the very few victories of Jewish forces over their oppressors. The holiday which celebrates the birth of Judaism as an organized faith is Passover and it might rank in importance with Christmas, although it bears no similarity to it.

**kháp-'n,** to catch

**kháp-'n bay der hant,** to catch red-handed

**kha-ró-te hób-'n,** to regret, to change one's mind

**khá-se-ne (di),** (Heb., *hatunah*), wedding

**khá-se-ne hób-'n,** to get married

**khá-se-ne mákh-'n,** to marry off

**khas ve-kho-lí-le,** (Heb., *has vehalilah*, mercy and forfend) God forbid

**khas ve-shó-l'm,** (Heb., *has veshalom*, mercy and peace), heaven forbid

**khá-v'r (der),** (Heb., *haver*), friend (masc.)

**khá-v'r-te (di),** (Heb., *haverah*), friend (fem.)

**khá-ye (di),** (Heb., *hayah*), beast, wild animal

**khá-z'n (der),** (Heb., *hazzan*), cantor

**khá-z'n-te (di),** wife of the cantor

**khá-z'r (der),** (Heb., *hazir*), swine; glutton, greedy one

**kha-zer-áy (dos),** (Heb., root, *hazir*, lit., pig-stuff); junk, cheap merchandise, junk food

**khém-i-ye (di),** chemistry

**khes,** the eighth letter of the Hebrew (and Yiddish) alphabet: ח, pronounced as is the two letter combination in German *ch*; in Yiddish *kh* (See Introduction)

**khésh-b'n (der),** (Heb., *heshbon*), account, bill, inventory

**khésh-v'n,** (Heb., *heshvan*), second month of Hebrew calendar

**khe-só-r'n (der),** (Heb., *haser*, missing), defect, shortcoming, fault

**khév-re (di),** (Heb., *hevrah*), group, gang, fellows

**khév-re-man (der),** one of the boys, tough guy, gangster

**khéy-der (der),** (Heb., *heder*), room; the one room school where male children of eastern Europe received their religious education. Under the tutelage of their teacher (See **melamed**), they began with the study of the Hebrew alphabet at the age of three and progressed through the prayer book (See **sider**), the Pentateuch (See **khumesh**), then on to the commentaries of the Talmud at the age of 12 or 13. Girls, generally, did not attend *kheyder* but learned to read at home, in between helping with the household chores.

**kheyn (der),** (Heb., *hen*), charm

**khéy-shek (der),** (Heb., *heshek*), will, desire, lust

**khi-rúrg (der),** surgeon

**khmál-ye (der),** blow, slap, punch

**khmá-re (di),** cloud, gloom

**khof,** the eleventh letter of the Hebrew (and Yiddish) alphabet: כ, pronounced as is the two letter combination *ch* in German; *kh* in Yiddish (See Introduction). When used at the end of a word the letter is printed: ך.

**khó-khem (der),** (Heb., *kakham*), wise one

**khó-khem éy-ner,** wise guy, idiot!

**khó-lem (der),** (Heb., *halom*), dream, hope

**kho-le-móyd,** (Heb., *hol hamoed*), intermediate days of the *peysakh* and *sukes* festivals.

**khó-lé-ri-ye (di),** cholera; harridan, fishwife, bitch

**kho-lí-le,** forfend, heaven forbid

**khó-luts (der),** (Heb., *halutz*), pioneer

**khó-mets (der),** (Heb., *hametz*), leaven; any food prohibited on Passover because it contains some taint of leaven

**khó-sid (der), kh'-sí-dim (di),** [Heb., *hasid* (sing.), *hasidim* (plu.)] , pious one(s), followers(s), adherent(s), fan(s). Most commonly refers to adherents of a mystical religious movement in Judaism which evolved in the 18th century in eastern Europe. It taught the value and appreciation of the joy of existence and love for the Almighty and for His children. It sought to replace the austerity of the fear of the Lord with devotion, trust, and joy. This was in direct opposition to the prevailing concepts of the time that study, fasting, austere prayer, and the ascetic life were most praiseworthy and acceptable to God. *kh'sidim* banded together under the leadership of a charismatic rabbi (See **rebe**), who often passed on his authority to a son, or son-in-law, creating an enduring dynasty. Such rabbis and their followers were located in the towns, villages, and cities of Poland and the Ukraine. Their followers still thrive in large metropolitan centers in the United States, Great Britain, and in

Israel, where descendants of most of the best known east European dynasties
are represented.

**khó-s'n (der)**, (Heb., *hatan*), groom, betrothed, suitor

**khó-s'n bréy-shis,** (Heb., *hatan b'reshit*), the honor of being called first to bless
the Torah in the synagogue on the festival of *simhat torah* (See **simkhes
toyre**) on which the Torah reading cycle of the year is begun anew with the
first chapter of Genesis, *b'reyshis.*

**khó-s'n tóy-re,** (Heb., *hatan torah*), the honor of being called last to bless the
Torah in the synagogue on the festival of *simhat torah* (See **simkhes toyre**)
when the reading cycle of the past year is concluded with the final chapter of
Deuteronomy, *d'vorim.*

**khotsh,** at least, although

**khóy-le (der),** (Heb., *holeh*) sick person, invalid

**khóy-shekh (der),** (Heb., *hoshekh*), darkness, gloom, black of night.

**khoyv (der),** (Heb., *hovah*), debt

**khóy-zik mákh-'n,** to make fun of, to deride

**kh'-réyn (der),** horseradish

**khróp-'n,** to snore

**khú-mesh (der),** (Heb., *humash,* five), Five Books of Moses, Pentateuch

**khú-pe (di),** (Heb., *hupah*), wedding canopy

**khúr-b'n (der),** (Heb., *hurban*), destruction, desolation, holocaust

**khush (der),** (Heb., *hush*), feeling, sense

**khúts-pe (di),** (Heb., *hutzpah*), impudence, unmitigated gall, effrontery

**khúts-pe-dik,** impertinent

**khvál-ye (di),** wave

**kí-bed (der),** (Heb., *kibud*), hospitality, refreshment, respect, honor

**kí-bits (der),** wisecrack, needle, joke

**kí-bits-'r (der),** onlooker, meddler, spectator who gives unsolicited advice; comedian

**kí-dish (der),** (Heb., *kiddush*), sanctification. Sabbaths and festivals are sancti-
fied and inaugurated by the recital of *kidish*, an invocation over a cup of wine,
symbol of God's providence, as an introduction to the festive meal. The
*kidish* for all such occasions follows the same general format except for the
addition of a number of appropriate phrases referring to the specific occasion
and to its significance. In a broader sense, *kidish* includes all refreshments
served in celebration of a festive religious occasion.

**kí-dish-a-shem,** (Heb., *kiddush hashem*), sanctification of the name of God;
martyrdom

**kikh (di),** kitchen

**kíkh-'l (dos),** cookie

**kil,** cool

**kím-'l (der),** caraway seed

**kin (di),** chin

**kind (dos),** child

**kínd-er-gort-'n,** kindergarten

**kínd-er yór-'n (di),** childhood

**kín-e (di),** (Heb., *kinah*), envy, jealousy

**kí-shef (der),** (Heb., *kishuf*), magic, mystical spell

**kí-she-le (dos),** little pillow

**kísh-ke (di),** intestine, gut, stuffed derma

**kísh-'n (der),** pillow, cushion

**kís-lev,** (Heb., *kislev*), third month of the Hebrew calender. Hanukkah (See
     **khanike)** falls on the 25th and continues for eight days.

**kítsl-en,** to tickle

**kí-yum (der),** (Heb., *kiyum*), survival

**klas (der),** class

**kláyb-'n,** to choose, to select

**klék-'n,** to suffice, to last

**klén-er,** smaller

**klér-'n,** to think, to wonder

**kleyd (dos),** dress

**kléyd-ung (di),** clothing, garb

**kley kóy-desh (di),** (Heb., *klei kodesh*, sacred vessels.) Jewish religious function-
     aries: *rov*, rabbi; *khaz'n*, cantor; *shamesh*, beadle; *shoykhet*, ritual slaughterer;
     *moyl*, ritual circumcizer

**klér-'n,** to think

**kleyn,** small

**kleyt (di),** store, shop

**kléz-mer (der),** (Heb., *klei zemer*, musical instruments), musician (instrumen-
     talist)

**klí-pe (di),** (Heb., *klipah*, rind, shell), nag, horse, hag, shrew

**klóg-'n,** to mourn, to weep

**klor,** clear, sane

**klots (der),** wooden beam, butcher block; clumsy, uncoordinated, crude person

**klots ká-she (di),** (Heb., root, *kushiyah*, question), simplistic, obvious, am-
     biguous or hypothetical question

**klóy-mersht,** (Heb., *k'lomar*, that is to say), apparently, as it were

**klóys-ter (der),** church

**klug,** clever, smart, intelligent

**k'mat,** (Heb., *k'm'at*), almost, approximately

**knák-er (der),** (lit., one who cracks or snaps); big shot
**knák-nis'l (dos),** nutcracker
**knékh-k'l (dos),** ankle
**knéy-d'l (dos),** matzah ball
**kneytsh (der),** crease, fold, skin line
**k'ni (der),** knee
**knip (der),** pinch, knot
**kníp-'l (dos),** (lit., little knot), small cache of money, a little put away for a rainy day
**knish (der),** pastry dumpling filled with potatoes, buckwheat groats, or meat
**knób-'l (der),** garlic
**kohen,** See **koyn**
**kókh-a-leyn (der),** (lit., to cook for one's self.) Summer cottages where vacationers do their own housekeeping, cooking, etc., in contrast to resort hotels where these services are performed by the staff.
**kókh-lef-'l (dos),** (lit., cooking spoon); busybody
**kókh-'n,** to cook
**kól-di-re (di),** blanket, comforter
**ko-lír (der),** color
**kól-ner (der),** collar
**kol níd-re,** (Heb., *kol nidre*, All vows . . . ), legal formula which opens the 24 hour fast of *yom kiper*, the Day of Atonement. It declares that all vows made rashly during the year and not fulfilled are null and void. Because it is recited at the beginning of the *yom kiper* eve service, the entire evening service is commonly referred to as the *kol nidre* service.
**kó-mik-er (der),** comic, comedian
**kom-pót (der),** fruit dessert
**ko-mu-níst (der),** communist
**kon-ku-rént (der),** competitor, adversary
**kon-vért (der),** envelope
**kop (der),** head
**kórb-'n (der),** (Heb., *korban*, sacrificial offering), victim
**kó-rev (der),** (Heb., *karov*, near one), relative
**kó-rik (der),** cork
**korn (der),** rye grain
**kórt-'n (di),** playing cards
**kosher,** See **kosh'r**
**kó-sh'r,** (Heb., *kasher*, clean), anything which may be eaten or is suitable for use according to Jewish law; also legal, above board
**kot-lét (der),** hamburger, cutlet

**kó-tsef (der),** (Heb., *katzef*), butcher

**kótsh-e-kes mit lá-pe-tes,** (lit., pokers and paddles); scrawled or illegible handwriting

**kóy-akh (der),** (Heb., *koah*), strength, vigor

**koyl (di),** bullet

**koym,** almost

**kóym-en (der),** chimney

**koyn (der), koy-há-nim (di),** (Heb., *kohen*), member(s) of the ancient priestly caste; now, descendants of that caste. Jews derive from three sources and are so designated for religious purposes. Those descended from the families of Moses and Aaron (who were members of the tribe of Levi), became the priests, the spiritual overseers and leaders in the rituals of the Holy Temple in Jerusalem, the chief officiants in the rites of the sacrificial codes. The rest of the tribe of Levi and their descendants, became Levites (See **leyvi, leviyim**), who assisted the priests in their Temple duties. The third group, Israelites, consists of the descendants of all the rest of the tribes and constitutes the major part of the congregation of Israel. The designations are passed on from father to son and continue to this day. Very little ritual responsibility is connected with each group today. A *koyn* is called first to bless the Torah; a *leyvi* is called next, and the remaining honors are distributed among the Israelites, *yisroeylim*. The *koyn* may also be called upon to officiate in the ceremony of Redemption of the First Born Son (See **pidyon habeyn**). He must also observe special restrictions in choice of a bride and in attending the dead.

**kóy-ne (der),** (Heb., *koneh*), customer, purchaser

**kramf (der),** cramp

**krank,** sick

**kráts-'n,** to scratch, to itch

**kra-vát (der),** tie

**krekhts (der),** sigh; a modest vocal response to some real or imagined pain or unpleasantness; usually preceded or followed by "oy!"

**krenk (di),** disease, illness

**krép-lakh (di),** boiled or fried dumplings filled with cheese or meat

**krig (di),** war

**kríg-'n,** to receive

**kríg-'n zikh,** to argue, to fight

**kríkh-'n,** to crawl

**kríkh-'n oyf á-le fir,** to crawl on all fours; a supreme effort

**kríkh-'n oyf di gláy-khe vent,** (lit., to crawl up the walls); an expression of extreme anguish or pain. Sometimes heard as picturesque malediction: *zollst krikh'n oyf di glaykhe vent,* Go climb the walls!

krist (der), Christian, gentile

krí-tish, critical, serious

krí-zhes (di), lower back (kidney) area

krom (der), store

kroyt (dos), cabbage

krum, crooked, crippled, lame

k'sú-be (di), (Heb., *ketubah*), wedding contract written and witnessed prior to the ceremony in which the groom agrees to provide certain rights, protection, and affection. According to Jewish law, bride and groom may not live together unless the bride has the *k'sube* in her possession.

ku (di), cow; also, stupid person

kuf, the nineteenth letter of the Hebrew (and Yiddish) alphabet: ק, pronounced as is the letter *k*.

kúg-'l (der), (Heb., root, *k'ugal*, round), pudding, usually potato, or noodle

kúk-'n, to look

kúk-'n ún-ter di nég-'l, (lit., to inspect fingernails); to watch very carefully, to scrutinize; to be on someone's back

kúm-en, to arrive

kúm-en óyf-'n séy-kh'l, (Heb., *sekhel*, good sense), to come to one's senses

kúm-en tsu khó-lem, (Heb., *halom*, dream), to appear in a dream

kunst (di), art

kúr-ve (di), whore

kush (der), kiss

ku-zín (der), cousin (masc.)

ku-zín-e (di), cousin (fem.)

k'vél-en, to enjoy, to take delight in

kvetsh (der), habitual complainer, sour-faced, malcontent

kvétsh-'n, to pinch, to squeeze, to press tightly, to paw

kvítsh-'n, to scream

# L

**la-dí-no,** the folk tongue derived from Spanish and Hebrew elements, spoken by Sephardic Jews who come primarily from the European countries which ring the Mediterranean, and from the Middle East.

**lág-er (der),** military, penal, or concentration camp

**lákh-'n,** to laugh

**lákh-'n mit yásh-tshe-kes,** (lit., to laugh with lizards); laughter through tears, unhappy laughter

**lám-d'n (der),** (Heb., *lamdan*), scholar in sacred studies

**lá-med,** the twelfth letter of the Hebrew (and Yiddish) alphabet: ל , pronounced as is the letter *l.*

**lánds-man (der),** countryman, compatriot, one who came from the same home town

**lá-te (di),** patch

**lát-ke (di),** pancake, usually of grated potatoes fried in oil; a special favorite on *khanike*

**láyd-'n,** to suffer

**láykht-er (der),** candlestick, candelabra

**láy-lakh (der),** bed sheet

**láy-tish,** decent, honorable, proper

**láy-tish ge-lékh-ter,** derision, stultification, making a foolish impression

**láy-v'nt (dos),** linen

**lé-be-dik,** lively, alive

**léb-'n (dos),** life

**léb-n,** beside, near

**léb-'n in dir,** (lit., life to you), expression of approval

**léb-'n ge-blíb-'n-er (der),** survivor

**léb-'r (di),** liver (anat.)

**lé-f'l (der),** spoon

**lég-'n zikh in der leng un der breyt,** (lit., to lie down in the length and width); to go all out, to spare no effort

**lé-kakh (der),** (Heb., *lekah*, teaching), cake; usually, honey cake

**le-khá-yim!,** (Heb., *lehayim*), to life!, to your good health!

**lék-tsi-ye (di),** lesson, assignment, lecture

**lé-mish-ke (di),** porridge; a milquetoast, spineless person, faint-hearted

**lém-p'l (dos),** electric bulb

**lér-er (der),** teacher

**lets (der),** comic, wag, jester

**le-vó-ne (di),** (Heb., *levanah*), moon

**léy-dik,** empty

**léy-di-gey-er (der),** idler, loafer, unemployed person

**léyg-'n,** to put away, to lay on, to lay down

**léyg-'n t'fí-lin,** (Heb., *tefilin*, prayers, phylacteries), to put on phylacteries

**léy-ken-en,** to deny

**léy-vi, le-ví-yim,** Levite(s). The Levites, descendants of the tribe of Levi, served in the Temple as administrators and managers, as singers in the Temple choir and as instrumentalists in the Temple orchestra. Like the *koyhanim* (Temple priests), the *leviyim* were given no land inheritance in Palestine and subsisted on the sacrifices and offerings brought to the Temple by the people. A *leyvi* is called to the *toyre* after the *koyn*. Today, the *leyvi* has no special religious responsibilities (see **koyn**).

**lib,** beloved, dear

**líb-e (di),** love

**lib hób-'n,** to love, to be fond of

**líb-hob-'r (der),** lover (man)

**lid (dos),** song, poem

**líg-'n (der)** lie, fabrication

**líg-'n,** to lie (as on a bed)

**likht béntsh-'n,** to kindle the Sabbath or festival lights with the appropriate blessing; generally, the responsibility of the woman of the house, although not limited to her.

**li-kó-ved,** (Heb., *likh'vod*), in honor of

**li-mó-sh'l,** (Heb., *limashal*), for example

**link,** left

**línk-er (der),** radical

**li-vá-ye (di),** (Heb., *levayah*), funeral cortege. Tradition considers it meritorious to escort the dead to their final resting place.

**lokh (der),** hole

**lokh in kop (der),** hole in the head

**lók-sh'n (di),** noodles

**ló-mir,** let us

**lósh-'n (der),** (Heb., *lashon*, tongue), language

**ló-sh'n hó-re (dos),** (Heb., *lashon hara*), gossip, vilification

**lóyf-'n,** to run

**lóyn-en,** to be worthwhile

**loyt,** according to

**lóz-'n,** to allow

**lóz-'n zikh bét-'n,** to be coy, to wait to be asked

**l'shó-ne tóy-ve,** (Heb., *l'shannah tovah*), a happy new year!

**lú-akh (der),** (Heb., *luah*), calendar. The Jewish calendar is a lunar calendar, adapted in ancient times from the Babylonians. Based upon the rotation of the moon around the earth, each new month is marked by the appearance of a new moon. The moon's trip around the earth takes 29½ days, therefore, the months of the Hebrew calendar are either of 29 or 30 days duration. This means that a lunar year is 354 days long. In order to make up the difference between that and the 365 day solar year, seven extra months are intercalated in the calendar every 19 years. The leap year month is added after the regular twelfth month, *oder* and is called *oder sheyni.* In a leap year, the festival of Purim, which falls on the 14th of *oder*, is celebrated during the extra month, *oder sheyni.* In addition to listing the days and months, the *luakh* usually contains additional vital information: sunset times for Sabbath eve, the weekly readings from the Pentateuch and the Prophets, the exact time of the appearance of the first sliver of the new moon, as well as the holidays and fast days.

**luft (di),** air, breath

**lúft-mensh (der),** (lit., air person.) One without visible means of support; a dreamer, an impractical person

**lú-lev (der),** (Heb., *lulav*), palm branch used in thanksgiving ritual during the festival of *sukes.* See **esrig.**

**lung (di),** lung

# M

**máb-'l (der)**, (Heb., *mabul*), flood

**ma-géy-fe (di)**, (Heb., *magefah*), pestilence

**má-ke (di)**, (Heb., *makah*), plague, wound, trouble, boil

**má-kher (der)**, (lit., one who makes); big shot, one with real or pretended authority

**ma-khe-rá y-ke (di)**, contraption, device

**ma-khe-shéy-fe (di)**, (Heb., *mahshefah*), witch, hag

**má-kh'n**, to make, to manufacture

**má-kh'n an ón-shtel**, to pretend, to put up a front

**má-kh'n a tsí-mes**, (lit., to make a pudding or stew), to bother, to make a fuss

**má-kh'n a tú-m'l**, to make noise, or a commotion

**mákh-'n shá-bes**, to prepare for the Sabbath

**mákh-z'r (der)**, (Heb., *mahzor*), holiday prayer book

**má-lakh (der)**, (Heb., *malakh*), angel

**má-lakh-a-mó-ves (der)**, (Heb., *malakh hamavet*), angel of death

**má-le zayn**, (Heb., root, *milah*), to circumcise (See **bris**)

**mál-ke (di)**, (Heb., *malkah*), queen

**mál-pe (di)**, monkey

**má-me lósh-'n**, mother tongue, plain talk

**mám-z'r (der)**, (Heb., *mamzer*), bastard

**man (der)**, man

**mánd-l'n (di)**, almonds; tonsils

**ma-nish-tá-ne**, (Heb., *mah nishtanah*), opening words of the Four Questions posed by the youngest at the Passover *seyder*—which motivate the retelling of the story of the Exodus from Egypt. The questions begin with: How different is this night from all other nights of the year? The questioner goes on to enumerate four differences between this meal and every other meal of the year and asks for an explanation.

In a secular context, difficult or odd questions are referred to as: questions from the *manishtana*.

**mán-t'l (der)**, overcoat

**ma-pó-le (di)**, (Heb., *mapalah*), downfall, defeat, disaster

**ma-ránts (der)**, orange (fruit)

**má-riv**, (Heb., *maariv*, evening service; also west), the evening service, recited after sunset each day. Tradition bids a Jew pray three times each day (additional times on Sabbath and holidays), morning, afternoon, and evening.

**47**

*mariv* may be recited anytime after sundown till late evening (See **minkhe, shakhris**).

**mark (der)**, market

**marts**, March

**má-ser-'n**, to denounce, to inform on

**ma-shín (di)**, car, auto, machine of any type

**más-kim zayn**, (Heb., root, *haskamah*, agreement), to agree

**mat-béy-e (di)**, (Heb., *matbeah*), coin, money

**mat-e-má-tik (di)**, mathematics

**mát-kes (di)**, underpants

**ma-tó-ne (di)**, (Heb., *matanah*), gift

**mat-rí-akh zayn**, (Heb., *matriah*), to trouble, to take the trouble

**má-tse (di)**, (Heb., *matzah*), unleavened "bread" eaten on Passover to commemorate the hurried departure of the Israelites from Egypt. Containing only flour and water, *matse* must be baked immediately after mixing the ingredients, the entire process taking no more than 18 minutes so that the natural leavening process shall not take place.

**má-tse bray (di)**, omelet made with *matse*

**mats-lí akh zayn**, (Heb., *matsliah*), to succeed

**matsoh**, See **matse**

**may**, May

**máy-kh'l (dos)**, (Heb., *maakhal*), foodstuff, tasty dish, treat

**máy-le (di)**, (Heb., *maalah*, virtue), asset, virtue, merit

**mayn bó-bes dáy-ge**, (Heb., *daagah*, problem, worry, lit., my grandmother's problem); I couldn't care less

**máy-se (di)**, (Heb., *maaseh*), story

**má-z'l (dos)**, (Heb., *mazal*), good luck; fate

**má-z'l-dik**, lucky, fortunate

**má-z'l tov**, (Heb., *mazal tov*), good luck! congratulations!

**mé-b'l**, furniture

**me-di-tsín (di)**, medicine, drug

**méd-resh (der)**, (Heb., *midrash*), collection of parables, allegories, legends, myths which serve to amplify, explain and comment upon the Bible and Talmud. Usually used as a homiletic aid by preachers and teachers. Refers either to a single item or to the entire collection.

**me-gí-le (di)**, (Heb., *megillah*, scroll), id., a long, detailed story

**me-gí-les Eś-ter**, (Heb., *Megillat Ester*), Biblical Scroll of Esther

**még-'n**, to be permitted

**me-há-lakh (der)**, (Heb., root, *halokh*), walk, a healthy distance

**me-ká-b'l (der)**, (Heb., *mekabel*, recipient), charity case, welfare recipient me-ká-ne zayn, (Heb., *mekaneh*), to be jealous, to envy

me-khá-bed, (Heb., *mekhabed*), the act of giving one an honor

me-khá-b'r (der), (Heb., *mekhaber*), author

me-khá-ye, (Heb., *mekhaye*, revives), a pleasure; an expression of approval

me-khe-té-nes-te (di), (Heb., *mehutan*, related by marriage), in-law (fem.)

me-khe-téy-se, (Aramaic, *mehai teti*, let come what will); all right, agreement with mild overtones of demural; i.e., all right, if that's the way you feel.

me-khí-t'n (der), in-law (masc.)

me-khú-le, (Heb., *mekhulah*, lost, ended), gone wrong, out of order, failed, bankrupt

mék-ler (der), broker

mel (di), flour

me-lá-med (der), (Heb., *melamed*), teacher of religious subjects (See **lerer**)

me-lá-ve mál-ke (di), [Heb., *melaveh malkah*, lit., to escort the queen (Sabbath)]. In Jewish folklore the Sabbath is referred to as Queen Sabbath. Tradition considers it meritorious to extend the duration of the Sabbath to its fullest possible limits. Pious Jews will tarry over the final Sabbath hours singing hymns (See **z'mires**) and prayer songs, above and beyond what the ritual for the closing of the Sabbath requires (See **havdole**) thus delaying her departure. The custom of extending the Sabbath by prolonging the process of leave taking.

me-lón (der), melon

mem, the thirteenth letter of the Hebrew (and Yiddish) alphabet: מ, pronounced as is the letter *m*. When it comes at the end of a word, it is printed: ם.

me-ná-khem ó-v'l zayn, (Heb., *menahem avel*, to comfort a mourner), to console a mourner, to pay a condolence call

me-nóy-re (di), (Heb., *menorah*), candelabra

mentsh (der), person, human being; a decent person

mén-t'l (dos), embroidered mantle for Torah scrolls

mer, more

mér-'n (di), carrots

mes (der), corpse

mé-ser (der), knife

me-shí-akh (der), (Heb., *mashiah*), the Redeemer who will bring salvation to the world at the end of days. Tradition has it that he will be a descendant of the house of David.

me-shí-akhs tsáyt-'n, (Heb., *mashiah*, Messiah), Messianic days, end of days

me-shu-gás (dos), (Heb., *meshugah*), madness, phobia

me-shú-ge, (Heb., *meshugah*), mad, insane, crazy, id., outlandish, bizarre

me-shú-ge-ner (der), madman

**me-shú-med (der)**, (Heb., *meshumad*), apostate; obstinate, contrary, person

**mes-tá-me,** (Aramaic, *mistama*), probably, perhaps

**me-tsí-ye (di)**, (Heb., *metziah*, lit., the find), bargain, good deal; cynically, to mean the opposite

**méy-b'l (di)**, furniture

**méy-d'l (dos)**, young girl, virgin, maiden

**me-yí-khes (der)**, (Heb. root, *yichus*, privilege), one who demands special attention and/or privileges

**méy-lakh (der)**, (Heb., *melekh*), king

**méy-nung (der)**, opinion, point of view

**méy-sim (die)**, (Heb., *met*), the dead

**méy-vin (der)**, (Heb., *mevin*, one who understands), connoisseur, expert

**me-zí-nik (der)**, youngest son

**me-zín-ke (di)**, youngest daughter

**me-zú-men (dos)**, (Heb., *mezuman*), cash, money, funds; also the three men quorum required to recite the Grace after meals in congregational fashion

**me-zú-ze (di)**, (Heb., *mezuzah*, doorpost). The Bible commands each Jew to place a parchment scroll on which is inscribed Israel's ancient credo, "Hear, O Israel, the Lord our God, The Lord is One," as a visible symbol of his faith and as a reminder of the conduct required of him by that faith. The scroll, containing two sections from Deuteronomy, is enclosed in a protective case and is placed on the right doorpost of each door in the house.

**mid,** tired

**míd-b'r (der)**, (Heb., *midbar*), desert

**mí-es,** ugly, disgusting, unbecoming

**mík-ve (di)**, (Heb., *mikvah*, well or pool), ritual bath used mainly by married women for purification following each menstrual period. Also used in purification rite for converts to Judaism.

**milkh (di)**, milk

**mílkh-ik,** foods containing dairy substances

**mil-khó-me (die)**, (Heb., *milhamah*), war, battle

**mil-khó-me hált-'n,** to wage war

**milts (di)**, spleen

**mil-yón (der)**, million

**mín-ter-'n,** to revive

**mir,** to me

**mi-sá-der ki-dú-sh'n (der)**, (Heb., *mesader kidushin*), generic term for one who officiates at a wedding; usually a rabbi or hazzan, although, insofar as Jewish law is concerned, it may be a learned and knowledgeable layman.

**mí-se me-shú-ne (di)**, (Heb., *mitah meshunah*), a violent death

**mi-she-béy-rekh,** (Heb., *mi sheberakh*, "May He who blessed our forefathers
. . .") opening words and title of a prayer formula used for petition or thanksgiving on behalf of particular named individuals. Usually recited by the
Reader (See **bal kerie**) during the time when the Torah scroll is read in the
synagogue; i.e., for the good fortune of a bride and groom about to be married; for the recovery of a person who is ill; for a safe journey for one about
to visit the Holy Land; in thanksgiving for someone who has attained a significant milestone; id., a dressing down, a harangue

**mísh-mash (der),** hodgepodge, clutter, confusion

**mísh-ne,** (Heb., *mishnah*), one of the two basic components of the Talmud; the
word derives from the Hebrew root, to study. The *mishne* was the first collection of Biblical commentary, and was organized into six prime categories.
It was compiled and edited by a distinguished group of scholars in Palestine,
under the direction of Judah the Prince, and completed in the year 200. It
represents the fruits of four centuries of religious scholarship (See **gemore**).

**me-shó-res (der),** (Heb., *misharet*), manservant, errand boy; id., stooge

**mis,** ugly

**mísh-pet (der),** (Heb., *mishpat*), judgement, verdict

**mish-pó-khe (di),** (Heb., *mishpahah*), family

**mish-téyns ge-zógt,** hardly, alas; used condescendingly or in pity; i.e., she calls
herself an actress, *mishteyns gezogt* (the poor thing thinks she's an actress).

**mis-káyt (dos),** ugly person, thing, or act

**mis-ná-ged (der),** (Heb., *mitnaged*, lit., opponent), primarily those rationalist
and traditionalist Jews who opposed Hasidism. They held that its preoccupa-
tion with joyfulness, with its unwavering belief in the mystical powers of the
hasidic *rebe* must bring with it a neglect of the study of the Torah, which in
the end would render a disservice to Judaism. In the 18th century, a deep
rift developed in many communities between the protagonists of the two
points of view; long-standing feuds developed which did not disappear entirely until the early 20th century. By now, excesses of both have greatly
diminished as has the animosity between the two factions. There are still
hasidim and those who do not hold with them, but the *misnaged* position is
passive and on a personal individual basis.

**mist (di),** dust

**mit á-le pítsh-ev-kes,** in full detail, full dress; with nothing left out

**mít-glid (der),** member

**mít-'l-shul (di),** high school

**mít-'n (der),** center

**mít-'n,** with

**mít-'n gánts-'n hárts-'n,** wholeheartedly

**mít-'n rékht-'n fis,** (lit., with the right foot). Appropriate encouragement for one beginning a new project, career, marriage, etc., i.e., May you begin well, in good fortune

**míts-ve (di),** (Heb., *mitsvah*), commandment, good deed

**míts-ve oyf im,** serves him right!, couldn't happen to a nicer guy!

**mít-vokh,** Wednesday

**míz-rakh (der),** (Heb., *mizrah*), east

**mó-de (di),** style, fashion

**mód-ne,** strange, peculiar, odd

**mó-ger,** lean, thin

**mó-g'n (der),** stomach

**mó-g'n dó-vid (der),** (Heb., *magen david*, shield of David), Star of David

**mo-mént (der),** moment

**mó-nat (der),** month

**món-tig,** Monday

**mór-g'n (der),** morning, tomorrow, future

**mó-sh'l (der),** (Heb., *mashal*), example, case in point

**móy-kh'l,** (Heb. root, *mohel*, to forgive), never mind, don't do me any favors

**móy-kh'l zayn,** (Heb. root, *mohel*, to forgive), to forgive

**moyl (dos),** mouth

**moyl (der),** (Heb., *mohel*), one authorized by training, knowledge and certification to perform a ritual circumcision

**móy-re (di),** (Heb., *morah*), fear

**móy-she ka-póyr,** upside down, backwards, cart in front of the horse; id., one who swims against the tide

**móy-shev z'kéy-nim (der),** (Heb., *moshav z'kenim*), old folks home

**móy-tse** (Heb., *hamotzi*), key word in the blessing over bread, which a traditional Jew recites before eating: Blessed art Thou, O Lord our God, King of the Universe who *brings forth* (*hamoytsi*) bread from the earth.

**moyz (di),** mouse

**m'-shó-res (der),** (Heb., *mesharet*), servant

**mú-me (di),** aunt

**mut (der),** courage, will

**mú-ter (di),** mother

**mú-tsh-'n,** to torment, to trouble, to tire, to bother

**mu-zík (di),** music

**mú-zik-er (der),** musician

# N

**nád-'n (der),** (Heb., *nadan*) dowry

**náf-ke (di),** prostitute

**naft (der),** petroleum, oil, gasoline, kerosene

**ná-khes (dos),** (Heb., *naḥat*, joy), reflected pleasure from the achievements of others

**nar (der),** fool

**nár-ish,** foolish

**nas,** wet

**nash (der),** snack

**nash-e-ráy (dos),** junk food

**násh-'n,** to snack, to feed a sweet tooth

**ná-yes (di),** news

**nayn,** nine

**náyn-tsik,** ninety

**náyn-ts'n,** nineteen

**né-bekh,** unfortunately, more's the pity

**né-bekh (der),** unfortunate or unhappy person; timid person; afraid of his own shadow

**nebish,** (See **nebekh**)

**ne-dó-ve (di),** (Heb., *nedavah*), donation, handout (See **tsedoke**)

**né-fish (der),** (Heb., *nefesh*), soul, human being; poor little thing

**ne-gí-dis-te (di),** wife of a wealthy man

**ne-kéy-ve (di),** (Heb., *nekevah*), female; sometimes, a female of low character

**ne-khó-me (di),** (Heb., *nehamah*), consolation

**nékht-i-ker tog (der),** (lit., yesterday's day); not at all, don't you believe it

**nékht-'n,** yesterday

**ne-kó-me (di),** (Heb., nekamah), revenge

**ném-en,** to take

**né-p'l (der),** fog

**ner tó-mid (der),** (Heb., *ner tamid*). Eternal Light. As a reminder of the ancient Temple in Jerusalem every synagogue has a lamp that burns continuously; usually suspended above the front of the Ark.

**nes (der),** (Heb., *nes*), miracle

**ne-shó-me (di),** (Heb., *neshamah*), soul

**neyn,** no

**nez'l (dos),** pug nose, little nose

**níd-rik,** low, cheap, vulgar

**ní-ef (der),** (Heb., *niuf*), adultery

**ní-g'n (der),** tune, melody

**ní-r'n (di),** kidneys

**nisan,** See **nis'n**

**nish-kó-she,** not bad

**nis-'n,** to sneeze

**ni-s'n,** (Heb., *nisan*), seventh month of Hebrew calendar. Passover begins on the fifteenth day and continues for eight days; outside of Israel; for seven days in Israel. *yom ha shoah,* the newly instituted memorial day for victims of the Holocaust, falls on the 27th day of the month.

**nit a-ráyn-ton a fín-ger in kalt vá-ser,** (lit., not to put a finger in cold water); not lift a finger, to loaf, to idle, to do as little as possible

**nit do ge-dákht,** let's not think of such (a possibility) here

**nit far-gín-en,** to begrudge, to envy

**nit ge-dáy-get,** don't worry!

**nit haynt ge-dákht,** id., of unhappy memory

**nit krank tsu,** it wouldn't hurt to . . .

**ni-tó,** absent, missing

**ni-tó far vús,** you are welcome, it's nothing

**nód-'l (di),** needle

**nó-ent,** near, nearby

**nó-gid (der),** (Heb., *nagid*), wealthy man

**nóg-l (der),** nail

**nokh a mol,** again, once again

**nókh-gey-en,** to follow

**nókh-makh-'n,** to ape, to imitate

**nokh-mí-tog (der),** afternoon

**nó-men (der),** name, title

**not'n (di),** musical notation

**nó-vi (der),** Heb., *navi*), prophet, forecaster

**noz (di),** nose, nostril

**nóz-tikh-'l (dos),** handkerchief

**nu,** well, so, get on with it

**núdg-'n,** to bother, to bore, to annoy, to pester

**núd-nik (der),** bore, pest

**nú-mer (der),** number; id., musical or literary selection

**nun,** the fourteenth letter of the Hebrew (and Yiddish) alphabet: נ , pronounced as is the letter *n*. When it comes at the end of a word it is printed: ן .

# O

**ó-ber,** but, however

**ó-der,** either, or

**ó-der,** (Heb., *adar*), sixth month of Hebrew calendar. Purim falls on the fourteenth day. In a Hebrew leap year an additional month, *oder II*, is added.

**ó-der-'n (di),** blood vessels

**ó-dom,** (Heb., *adam*), the first man, Adam; also used as a given name

**of,** awake

**of-'n,** open

**oft,** often, sometimes, occasionally

**o-léy-o-a-sho-l'm,** Heb., *aleha hashalom*), may she rest in peace

**ó-lov-a-sho-l'm,** (Heb., *alav hashalom*), may he rest in peace

**ó-meyn,** (Heb., *amen*), so be it. Proper response to the recitation of a benediction.

**on,** without

**on a só-fek,** (Heb., *safek*, doubt), without a doubt

**ón-fang-en,** to begin

**ón-ge-bloz-n,** surly, conceited, snobbish, angry, surly

**ón-ge-shtelt-er (der),** employee

**ón-ge-ton,** dressed

**ón-ge-ton in é-sik un in hón-ik),** (lit., dressed in vinegar and honey); dressed in one's best; dressed to the hilt

**ón-ge-tsoy-g'n,** (lit., wound up), angry, tense, up-tight

**ón-ge-zen,** famous, honored, important

**on khéy-shek,** (Heb., *heshek*, desire), without desire, reluctantly, listlessly

**ón-kum-en,** to arrive

**ón-nem-en,** to accept, to assume (duties, responsibilities, debts)

**ón-ri-r'n,** to touch

**ón-shik-e-nesh (dos),** affliction, nuisance, bolt out of the blue

**ón-ton,** to dress

**ón-ton zikh a máy-se,** (lit., to do one's self a deed); to commit suicide

**ón-tsind-'n,** to kindle, to switch on

**on zalts un on fé-fer,** (lit., without salt and pepper); dull, bland

**ón-zid'l-en,** to scold

**ón-zog-'n,** to instruct, to inform, to warn

**on zórg-'n,** to carefree, without any worries

**óp-geb-'n,** to give back, to report, to convey

**op-géb-'n má-z'l tov,** to congratulate

**óp-hit-'n**, to guard, to perform faithfully, to observe the commandments

**óp-khap-'n dem ó-tem**, to catch one's breath, to take a break

**óp-kling-en**, to telephone

**óp-kum-en**, to suffer through, to get it over with

**óp-lek-'n a béyn-d'l**, (lit., to lick a bone); to have a share in the profit or benefit; has a slightly uncomplimentary feeling about it, i.e., to enjoy benefits to which one is really not entitled, to take a cut of the loot

**óp-leyg-'n**, to postpone

**óp-loz-'n**, to dismiss, to fire

**óp-nar-'n**, to deceive, to cheat

**óp-ruf-'n**, to telephone, to respond

**óp-ruf-'n zikh**, to speak up, to be heard from, to give an opinion, to respond

**óp-sher-'n**, to cut (with scissors)

**óp-shprekh-'n**, to exorcise

**óp-ti-ker (der)**, optometrist

**óp-tret (der)**, outhouse, toilet

**óp-tret-'n**, to retreat, to withdraw

**ó-rem**, poor

**o-re-mán (der)**, pauper

**ó-rem-kayt (di)**, poverty

**or-gás-'m (der)**, orgasm

**ór-g'l (der)**, organ (musical)

**ó-r'n (der)**, chest, cabinet, coffin

**ó-r'n koy-desh (der)**, (Heb., *aron hakodesh*), holy ark; the cabinet where the Torah scrolls are kept in the synagogue

**ort (dos)**, place, seat

**ot**, there, aha!

**ó-tem (der)**, breath

**ó-tem-en**, to breathe

**ot, ot**, almost, on the verge of, on the brink

**ov**, (Heb., *av*), eleventh month of the Hebrew calendar. The three week period of mourning for the destruction of the Temple, in 70 of the Common Era, which begins on the seventeenth of the previous month of *tomiz*, concludes on the ninth day of *ov*, *tishe b'ov*.

**ó-ves (di)**, forefathers

**ó-v'l (der)**, mourner, bereaved one

**ó-v'nt (der)**, evening

**oyb**, if

**óy-ber-flekh-likh**, superficial

**óy-ber-man-t'l (der)**, overcoat

óyb-'n on, up front

óy-er (der), ear

óy-er-ing-'l (der), earring; also, caustically to describe a calculating, scheming or strong willed woman; i.e., *zi iz a froy mit an oyering'l*, lit., she's a dame with an earring

oyf, upon

óyf-boy-en, to erect

oyf di shpits fíng-er, on tiptoe

óyf-ga-be (di), assignment, duty

óyf-halt-'n, to support

óyf-her-'n, to stop

óyf-heyb-'n, to lift

óyf-khap-'n zikh, to wake up

óyf-makh-'n, to open

óyf-munt-er-'n, to revive, to cheer up

óyf-'n (der), (Heb., *ofan*, manner), manner, way

óyf-'n kol, aloud

óyf-rays (der), explosion

oyf shpíl-kes, on pins and needles

óyf-shtel-'n, to erect

óyf-shtey-en, to arise, to stand up, to awaken

óyf-shtey-en oyf der línk-er zayt, to get up on the wrong side of the bed, in a foul mood

oyf tsó-res, (Heb., *tsarot*, troubles), in trouble, in need

oyf vus di velt shteyt, (lit., on the foundations of the earth); for all it's worth, the utmost effort, matter of life and death

oyg (der), eye

óyg-'n-dokt-er (der), oculist

óy-gust, August

oykh, also

óy-lem (der), (Heb., *olam*, world), crowd, audience, public

óy-lem há-be (der), (Heb., *olam haba*), world to come, eternity, Paradise

óy-lem há-ze, (Heb., *olam hazeh*), life in this world

óy-rekh (der), (Heb., *oreah*), guest

oys (der), (Heb., *ot*), letter of the alphabet

oys, over, out

óys-ar-bet-'n, to manufacture; to work out (an arrangement)

óys-bet-n, to have one's prayers answered; i.e., *ir zolt zikh oysbet'n a gut yor*, May your prayers for a good year be answered

óy-sen-vey-nig, by heart

óys-ge-dart, emaciated, withered
óys-ge-las'n, lewd, lascivious
óys-ge-mu-tshet, tormented, tired out, exhausted
óys-ge-putst, dressed up
óys-gey-en, to expire, to fade away, to die
óys-glitsh-'n, to slip
óys-halt-'n, to bear, to survive; to support
óys-her-'n, to hear out, to audition
óys-heyl-en, to heal, to cure
óys-ho-de-v'n, to rear, to bring up
óys-khap-'n, to grab, to snatch up
óys-klayb-'n, to choose, to select
óys-kler-'n, to invent, to think up
óys-krenk-'n, to use up one's assets in sickness
óys-lern-en, to learn
óys-leyz-'n, to ransom, to redeem
óys-mayd-'n, to avert, to thwart
óys-mek-'n, to erase
óys-nits-'n, to utilize
óys-shnayd-'n, to cut out, to delete
óys-tayn-en zikh, to explain, to debate
óys-teyl-en, to distribute
óys-ton zikh, to undress
óys-tseyl-en, to count out
óys-tsiy-en, to drag out, to expand
oys-tsol-en, to pay out, to pay off in installments
óys-vaks-'n, to grow up
óys-vash-'n, to launder
óys-vorf (der), ne'er-do-well, scoundrel, reprobate
óys-zey-en, to appear
óys-zog-'n, to disclose, to tattle
óy-tser (der), (Heb., *otsar*), treasure
ov vey, woe is me
óy-v'n (der), oven, stove

# P

**pad-ló-ge (di),** floor

**pak-'n,** to pack

**pa-mé-lakh,** slowly, carefully

**pa-pír (dos),** paper

**pa-pi-rós (der),** cigarette

**pá-re-ve,** (Heb., *parev*), neutral food which is derived neither from meat or dairy components (vegetables, fruit, etc.). Also, in the vernaculer, bland, not outstanding.

**pár'-kh (der),** (Heb., *parah*, sprout or flower), an unpleasant, scabby disease of the scalp, or one who suffers from it; also, an unsavory or shady character.

**par-nó-se (di),** (Heb., *parnasah*), livelihood, income

**pa-rúk (der),** toupe

**pás-ik,** fitting, appropriate

**pa-sí-rung (di),** event

**pás-ken-en,** (Heb., *p'sak*, judgement), to judge, to rule

**pás-ken-en a sháy-le,** to rule on a religious question, an authority restricted to an ordained rabbi

**pas-kúd-ne,** disgusting, rotten, bad tasting

**pas-kud-nyák (der),** a disgusting, unappetizing person, lout

**pás-tukh (der),** shepherd

**patsh (der),** slap

**pátsh-k'n,** to engage in a tedious or messy job

**pátsh-'n,** to slap, to applaud

**pa-yáts (der),** clown

**páy-nik-'n,** to torture, to oppress

**pe-désh-ve (di),** sole of a shoe or foot

**pék-'l tsó-res (dos),** parcel of troubles

**pelts (der),** fur, pelt

**pé-re-ne (di),** feather comforter

**pesah,** See **peysakh**

**péy-de (di),** wages, salary. Probably developed, by early east European immigrants, from pay-day

**péy-e (di),** (Heb., *peyah*, corner), earlock. Pious Jews allow their earlocks to grow in observance of the commandment: "You shall not clip your hair at the temples or mar the edges of your beard." Traditionally, earlocks must be long enough to reach the earlobes.

**péy-ger-'n,** to die; used only for animals, although in vernacular used to describe death of an unpopular or antisocial person.

**péy-sakh,** (Heb., *pesah*, from the root, to pass over.) Festival which celebrates the liberation of the ancient Hebrews from Egyptian bondage; observed for eight days (seven, in Israel), commencing on the fifteenth of the month of *nis'n*. Special dietary restrictions forbid the presence in the home or the partaking of any food containing leaven. On each of the first two nights, a *seyder* is conducted during which the story of the Exodus is retold in songs, prayers, hymns, and readings. The "bread of poverty," *matse,* unleavened wafer of flour and water, is the traditional food and symbol of the holiday.

**pínkt-lekh,** exactly, punctual

**písh-er (der),** one who urinates; a young upstart

**pisk (der),** mouth; used not only in the anatomical sense but also to denote a loudmouth, an articulate speaker, the gift of gab, i.e., *oy hot er a pisk,* Boy, has he got a mouth.

**píts-'l (dos),** tiny bit; also very young infant

**pi-yo-nír (der),** pioneer

**pláp-len,** to blabber

**plats (dos),** place, site, seat

**pláts-'n,** to explode, to burst

**pléts-'l,** flat roll; best known variety is the *byalistoker plets'l,* reputedly named after the great Polish Jewish community of Byalistok; commonly referred to as a *b'yaly.*

**pléy-tse (di),** shoulder, upper back

**plikh (der),** bald pate

**pli-mé-nik (der),** nephew

**pli-mé-ni-tse (di),** niece

**plúts-ling,** suddenly

**p'-néy (di),** (Heb., from the word *panim,* face), elite, upper class, important people

**pók-'n (di),** vaccination

**po-mi-dór (der),** tomato

**pó-nim (dos),** (Heb., *panim*) face

**pó-li-tse (di),** shelf

**po-li-tséy (di),** police

**pó-rets (der),** landowner, nobleman

**pór-'l (dos),** pair, couple

**pór-'n zikh,** to copulate

**post (di),** mail

**pót-ko-ve (di),** horseshoe

**pót-'r,** to be rid of, to end

**pots (der),** penis, id., stupid, insensitive, boor

**póy-er (der),** farmer

**poyk (di),** drum

**prés-'l (dos),** flatiron

**prí-tse (di),** noblewoman

**pri-vi-lég-i-ye (di),** privilege

**pró-be (di),** audition, rehearsal

**prost,** common, low character, uneducated, plain

**p'sak (der),** (Heb., *p'sak*), verdict, judgement

**púkh-ke,** fluffy

**pú-pik (der),** navel; chicken gizzard, (id., abdomen)

**pú-rim,** (Heb., *purim*, lots), Feast of Lots, celebrates the victory of the Jews of Persia over the arch-villain, Haman. As told in the Bible's Scroll of Esther, (See **me-gi-le**) Haman casts lots to decide upon a date for his planned massacre of the Jews of Persia. The heroine, Esther, and her uncle, Mordecai, manage to expose Haman's plot, and the fate which he had planned for the Jews of Persia befalls him and his sons. Purim is celebrated on the fourteenth of the month of *oder* with a public reading of the Scroll of Esther, eating *homentash'n*, pastry buns formed in the shape of Haman's ears, with the exchange of gifts and sweets and by distributing gifts to the poor.

**púsh-ke (di),** collection box

**pust,** empty, abandoned, deserted

**pust un pas,** idle, forlorn, wasted

**putz,** See **pots**

**pyá-te (di),** heel

# R

**rakh-mó-nes,** (Heb., *raḥmanut*), compassion, pity, mercy
**rá-te-v'n,** to rescue
**raykh,** rich, wealthy
**reb,** mister
**ré-be (der),** (Heb., *rabi*), teacher; also leader of a hasidic sect. The *rebe* of a hasidic sect is an ordained rabbi; the *rebe* who is simply a teacher of Jewish religious subjects need not be. The hasidic *rebe* may head a group of adherents of thousands; a *rebe*–teacher may be the instructor for a handful of young students (See: **kheyder**). Not to be confused with *rov* (Heb., *rav*) which is used exclusively as a title for an ordained rabbi qualified to preach, to teach, and to give decisions on questions of Jewish law.
**ré-de (di),** address, speech
**réd-ner (der),** speaker, orator
**re-fú-e (di),** (Heb., *refuah*), cure, healing, remedy
**ré-ge (di),** (Heb., *regah*), moment, second, instant
**re-gí-rung (di),** government
**re-g'n (der),** rain
**re-khí-les (dos),** (Heb., *rekhilut*), gossip, slander
**ré-khen-en,** to figure, to add, to compute, to charge
**rékh-nung (der),** inventory
**rekhts,** to the right
**resht (der),** rest, remainder
**ré-tekh (der),** radish
**re-tsépt (der),** prescription, recipe
**réy-akh (der),** (Heb., *reah*), aroma, odor, fragrance
**réy-d'n,** to speak
**réy-ge (di),** (Heb., *regah*), moment, second
**réy-g'n (der),** rain
**reyn,** pure, clean
**réyn-kayt (die),** purity, cleanliness
**reysh,** the twentieth letter of the Hebrew (and Yiddish alphabet: ר , pronounced as is the letter *r*.
**ri-bóy-ne shel óy-l'm (der),** (Heb., *ribono shel olam*). Master of the Universe
**ríkht-er (der),** judge
**ríkht-ik,** correct
**ríkht-'n zikh,** to expect, to anticipate, to prepare for

**rí-nen,** to leak
**rír-ev-dik,** agile, active
**rír-'n,** to move, either physically or emotionally
**rír-'n-dik,** moving, touching
**riz (der),** giant
**ro-mán (der),** novel, story
**ró-she-sho-ne,** (Heb., *rosh hashanah*), new year. By biblical command the new
  year is celebrated for two days, on the first and second day of the month of
  *tishrey*. It marks the anniversary of the creation of the world. The other
  biblical festivals are observed for one day in Israel and for two days else-
  where, according to the ancient formula of the rabbis to cover the uncer-
  tainties of early communications and calendar calculation. However,
  *rosheshone* is observed for two days, even in Israel, in response to the
  specific biblical instruction. Reform Jewry, nevertheless, observes the
  holiday for only one day.
    *tishrey*, the month in which *rosheshone* is celebrated, is the seventh month,
  and not the first, as might be expected. That is because tradition considers
  the month in which the Israelites were liberated from Egypt, *nis'n*, as the first
  of all the months, and the calendar is so constructed that *rosheshone* marks
  not the commencement of a national calendar year, but the commencement
  of a universal spiritual year.
    The holiday is marked by extended prayers for a good new year. It stresses
  the point that the new year offers each human being a fresh opportunity to
  begin anew, to determine to lead a better, more useful, more concerned life.
  The *shoyf'r*, the ram's horn, is sounded to awaken man to his shortcomings
  and to his responsibilities to God, to fellow man, and to himself. At home,
  Jews dip slices of apples into honey at mealtime, as an expression of their
  hope for a sweet new year. On the afternoon of the first day, observant Jews
  make their way to any nearby flowing body of water into which they
  symbolically cast their sins, in a ceremony called *tashlikh*, casting.
**rosh-khóy-desh,** (Heb., *rosh hodesh*), new month. The onset of a new month,
  coinciding with the appearance of the first sliver of a new moon is considered
  a special occasion and is marked by appropriate additions to the liturgy of
  the regular services for that day.
**ro-s'l-fleysh (der),** pot roast
**roy,** raw
**róy-akh (der),** smoke
**royt,** red
**róyt-er (der),** communist, radical
**ró-ze,** pink

**ró-zhin-ke (di),** raisin
**rud (der),** circle, wheel
**rúf-'n,** to call, to notify
**rú-ik,** calm, peaceful
**rú-k'n-beyn (der),** spine
**rú-s'l-flaysh (der),** pot roast

# S

**sakh-há-k'l (der)**, (Heb., *sakh hakol*), grand total

**sa-kó-ne (di)**, (Heb., *sakanah*), danger

**sa-kó-nes ne-fó-shes**, (Heb., *sakanut nefashot*), mortal danger

**sa-lát (der)**, lettuce

**sá-mekh**, the fifteenth letter of the Hebrew (and Yiddish) alphabet: ס , pronounced as is the letter *s*.

**sán-dik (der)**, (Heb., *sandek*), godfather at a circumcision, whose sole duty is to escort the male child to the ritual circumsizer (See **moyl, bris**).

**sáy-vi-say**, anyway, nevertheless

**se-fár-dim**, (Heb., *sefaradim*, Spaniards), Jews whose ancestors lived in the countries bordering the Mediterranean. *sefardim* represent one of the two cultural–religious streams which evolved in Judaism in the centuries following the destruction of the Second Temple and the Palestinian commonwealth. The other members of the dual constituency are the *ashkenazim* (Heb., *ashkenazim*, Germans), who settled in central and eastern Europe. *sefardim* are closer in life-style to the Arab culture, while *ashkenazim* favor European or western patterns. Each of the groups has its special customs, rituals, cultural identity, and liturgical style, but both are equally loyal adherents to Judaism, and share, in common, its sacred literature, commandments, and general worship and ritual observances.

**se-kún-de (di)**, second (in time)

**se-le-rí-ye (di)**, celery

**séy-der (der)**, (Heb., *seder*, order), the festive meal of the first two nights of Passover. In addition to the traditional unleavend food, there is a long and varied ritual by means of which the story of the Exodus from Egypt is retold. The order of the ritual, from which the occasion gets its name, the *seyder*, is prescribed in a manual or *seyder* book, called the *hagode* (the telling). It contains prayers, rituals, stories, hymns, prayers, and complete directions for the order of the *seyder*. Since it is a family affair, provision is made for young and old to participate (See **fir kashes, afikoymen, manishtane**).

**séy-fer (der)**, (Heb., *sefer*), book; used only in reference to sacred books.

**séy-fer tóy-re (der)**, (Heb., *sefer torah*, scroll of the Law), refers to the scroll on which is inscribed the text of the Pentateuch and which is read aloud in the synagogue on Sabbaths, festivals, and on Monday and Thursday mornings of each week. Written by hand by a scribe (See **soyfer**) with a feather quill on parchment made from a permitted (kosher) animal, and stored, when not in use, in the Holy Ark (See **or'n koydesh**) of the synagogue, it is usually adorned with a colorful cloth mantle, silver crown, and breast plate.

**séy-kh'l (der)**, (Heb., *sekhel*), wisdom, understanding, wit, discernment; common sense

**sha!**, be still!

**shá-bes (der)**, (Heb., *shabbat*), Sabbath

**shád-kh'n (der)**, (Heb., *shadkhan*), marriage broker, matchmaker

**shá-fe (di)**, closet, cabinet

**shá-mes (der)**, (Heb., *shamash*, servant), synagogue sexton or beadle; id., "gofor," straw boss

**shán-de (di)**, shame, embarrassment

**shár-b'n (der)**, skull

**sháy-t'l (dos)**, wig worn by Orthodox women in compliance with the law that requires a married woman to keep her natural hair covered in public to avoid tempting other men

**she-khe-yó-nu**, (Heb., *sheheheyanu*, ". . . who has kept us in life . . ."), blessing recited in thanksgiving for happy occasions; i.e., birthday, new clothes, first fruit or vegetable of a new season; added to liturgy of the opening night service on festivals.

**she-khí-te (di)**, (Heb., *shehitah*), ritual slaughter; cutting through the windpipe and gullet with a specially sharpened and honed knife; (see **shoykhet**) also, massacre

**shékht-'n**, to slaughter animals according to ritual (See **shoykhet**), id., to kill

**she-lí-akh (der)**, (Heb., *sheliah*), emissary, representative

**shélt-'n**, to curse

**shé-men zikh**, to be ashamed, embarrassed

**shém-ev-dik**, bashful, shy

**shenk (di)**, tavern

**shénk-'n**, to give away, to donate

**she-ví-es**, (Heb., *shavuot*, weeks), Feast of Weeks, falls seven weeks after Passover and celebrates the moment when the newly freed Hebrews stood at Mt. Sinai and received the Ten Commandments.

**shevuos**, See **shevies**

**shéy-gets (der)**, gentile (masc.)

**sheyn**, pretty, handsome, fine

**shéyn-e réyn-e ka-pó-re**, (lit., a beautiful, pure atonement). May this minor difficulty serve as vicarious atonement for a more serious one; also, serves him right!

**shéyn-er yid (der)**, fine Jew, God fearing, observant, knowledgeable

**shéyn-kayt (di)**, beauty, beautiful person

**shif (di)**, ship
**shí-ker (der)**, drunkard
**shí-ker**, to be drunk
**shík-'n**, to send
**shík-se (di)**, gentile (fem.)
**shík-ying-'l (der)**, messenger
**shin**, the twenty-first letter of the Hebrew (and Yiddish) alphabet: שׁ, pronounced as is the two-letter combination *sh*.
**shir (der)**, (Heb., *shiur*), limit
**shí-rem (der)**, umbrella
**shis-e-ráy (dos)**, exchange of shots, barrage
**shí-ve**, (Heb., *shivah*, seven), the seven days of mourning after burial observed by the family of the deceased (parents, children, siblings, mates). The bereaved sit on low stools and do not leave the house. They may do no work, not even the preparation of food; this is attended to by friends and neighbors. Mirrors are covered, mourners wear no leather shoes, men do not shave, women do not use cosmetics. Daily services are held in the home. Friends visit to extend condolences and to give mourners an opportunity to articulate their grief. *shive* is suspended on the Sabbath, since public mourning is not permitted on that day. When a death and burial occur immediately prior to a festival, *shive* is annulled. When death and burial occur during a festival, the entire seven day ritual is delayed until the conclusion of the festival.
**sh'-khéy-ne (di)**, (Heb., *shakhen*), neighbor (fem.)
**sh'-khí-ne (di)**, (Heb., *shekhinah*), the divine spirit, presence of God in the world
**shklaf (der)**, slave (masc.)
**shkláf-er-ay (dos)**, slavery
**shlak (der)**, stroke of bad luck, misfortune; also shaddy business or merchandise
**shlank**, slim, lithe, graceful
**shláy-kes (di)**, suspenders
**shlekht**, bad, evil, wrongdoing
**shle-máz-'l (der)**, bad luck, born loser (See **shlemil**)
**shle-míl (der)**, inept one, misfit, sad sack
**shlép-er (der)**, (lit., one who pulls); unlucky pauper, dogged by misfortune; bum, hobo, beggar
**shlís-'l (der)**, key
**shlít-'n (der)**, sleigh
**shlóf-'n**, to sleep
**shlóf-tsi-mer (der)**, bedroom
**shlóg-'n**, to hit, to slap, to punch
**shlóg-'n ka-pó-res**, to perform the pre-*yom kiper* scapegoat atonement ritual (See **kapores**).

**shlos (der),** lock

**shlóy-shim,** (Heb., *shloshim,* 30), first 30 days following a death and burial. Transitional mourning period in which the bereaved are helped to move from the intense grief of the first seven days (*shive*) to a more regular regimen. Mourners may leave the house of mourning, do their regular work, but still refrain from any pleasureable activity.

**shlump (der),** slattern, slob, dowdy person; used as a verb commonly in English, "to shlump around," to go around unkempt

**shmád-'n zikh,** to convert from Judaism to some other religion

**shmalts (der),** animal fat, usually chicken fat; also, oversentimentality, emotionalism, bathos

**shmálts-grib (der),** (lit., a pit filled with chicken fat); to fall into something soft, to hit the jackpot, to succeed by sheer luck

**shmá-te (di),** rag; anything of shabby quality, i.e., a poor play, a cheap dress

**shmék-'n,** to smell (inhale)

**shmek tá-bik (der),** (lit., a pinch of snuff); tiny bit, something of little value

**shmén-drik (der),** nobody, nincompoop

**shméy-kh'l (der),** smile

**shméy-kh'l-en,** to smile; to flatter, to butter up

**shmi-gé-ge (der),** dolt, fool, incompetent, hapless one

**sh'-mí-ni a-tsé-res,** (Heb., *sh'mini atzeret*). Eighth Day of Solemn Assembly, a one day festival which falls at the close of the seven day *sukes* holiday. *yizk'r* is recited in the synagogue, as is the special prayer for rain for Israel's rainy season about to commence.

**shmír-akhts (dos),** lotion, ointment

**shmír-kez (der),** cream cheese

**shmok (der),** penis; also, id., stupid, insensitive, boor

**shmol,** narrow, tight

**shmol hált-'n,** things are critical

**shmuck,** See **shmok**

**shmus (der),** conversation, chat

**shmuts (dos),** dirt, garbage

**shnaps (der),** whiskey

**shnáyd-er (der),** tailor

**shnáyd-er-ke (di),** seamstress

**shnáyd-'n,** to cut

**shney (der),** snow

**shnips (der),** bow-tie

**shnór-er (der),** beggar, cheap person, slow spender; collector for real or imagined charities

**shnuk (der),** (lit., elephant's trunk); nobody, easy mark, simpleton

**sho (di),** hour
**shód-'n (der),** damage
**shofar,** See **shoyfer**
**shó-kh-'n (der),** (Heb., *shakhen*), neighbor (masc.)
**shókl-'n,** to shake; to sway in fervent prayer
**shó-lesh sú-des,** (Heb., *shalosh seudot*), the third meal. Extra meal eaten on Sabbath afternoon, to distinguish it from other days of the week when only two meals were eaten each day. Actually, it is a very light meal, eaten after a Sabbath study hour, for which most Jews would save food from the other meals. The mood was a melancholy one, as the lengthening shadows brought with them reminders of the imminent departure of the Sabbath.
**shó-l'm (der),** (Heb., *shalom*) peace
**shó-l'm a-léy-khem,** (Heb., *shalom aleikhem*), lit., peace be with you). The greeting when one Jew meets another; the response is: *aleykhem shol'm*; also the name of a popular hymn of welcome to the Sabbath.
**shó-l'm bá-yis,** (Heb., *shalom bayit*), domestic bliss
**shos (der),** shot, blow, explosion, loud sound
**shót-'n (der),** shadow
**shóy-f'r (der),** (Heb., *shofar*), ram's horn. Ancient musical instrument which still survives. Used as part of the *rosheshone* ritual in the synagogue and to mark the conclusion of *yom kiper*. It calls man to awaken to his shortcomings and responsibilities. *shoyf'r* has a limited musical range; the few sounds it can make are accomplished by a change in the rigidity of the lips and tongue. In ancient times the *shoyf'r* was used in the Temple service and also to sound an alarm in times of danger or war, or to announce the Sabbath and festivals.
**shóy-khet (der),** (Heb., *shohet*), ritual slaughterer; must be expert in Jewish law, especially in matters pertaining to ritual slaughter. He must also be a pious and sensitive person who is fully aware of his awesome responsibility. He must be certified by the rabbis of his community as to his skill and knowledge.
**shpas (der),** joke
**shpa-tsír-'n,** to promenade, to saunter, to stroll
**shpáy-en,** to spit
**shpet,** late
**shpil (di),** game, show, performance
**shpíl-ke (di),** pin
**shpíl-en,** to play (games, instruments), a role
**shpi-nát (der),** spinach
**shpits (der),** point, end, summit, top

shpi-túl (der), hospital
shpó-g'l nay, brand new
shpór-'n, to save, cut down, economize; to do without
shpríkh-vert-'l (dos), saying, proverb
shpríng-en, to jump
shprits (der), spray, shower
shráyb-er (der), author, writer
shráyb-ma-shin (di), typewriter
shrek (der), fright, fear
shrék-lakh, terrible, terrifying
shroyf (der), screw, bolt
shróyf-'n-tsi-yer (der), screwdriver
shtárb-'n, to die
shtark, strong
shtárk-er (der), tough guy
shtayf, stiff, starched, rigid, haughty
shtayg (di), cage
shték-'n (der), stick
shték-shikh (di), houseslippers
shtél-e (di), job, position
shtér-en, to disturb
shter'n (der), star; also, forehead
shtét-'l (dos), village, hamlet, rural settlement, particularly those in which Jews
    lived in Czarist Russia. They settled in these out-of-the-way places because
    they were not permitted residence permits for the large cities. The *shtet'l*
    represents the site of a 500 year Jewish European culture.
shtéy-en, to stand
shteyn (der), stone
shtik (der), piece; also act, routine
shtik be-héy-me, (Heb., *behema*, domesticated animal, lit., a piece of cow);
    fool, half-wit
shtím-e (di), voice
shtím-en, to vote
shtív-'l (di), boots
shtok (der), story, upper floor
shtokh (der), prick, jibe, stitch
shtolts, proud
shtol-tsí-r'n, to take pride
shtot (di), city, town
shtoyb (der), dust

shtshav, soup made from fennel or spinach

shtub (di), house, home

shukh (der), shoe

shúkh-bend-lakh (di), shoelaces

shul (di), synagogue

shuld (di), blame, fault

shúld-ik, guilty, to blame

shúl-e (di), school

shúl-kh'n ó-rekh (der), (Heb., *shulhan arukh*, the set table). The 16th century compendium of Jewish law divided into parallel categories to the *mishne*, edited by Joseph Caro, great Sephardi scholar. Culled from the Talmud and other sources, it represents the authoritative table of laws observed by pious Jews. Similar collections were prepared by other qualified scholars; none of them, however, equaled the *shulkh'n orekh* in popularity.

shtoys (der), poke

shtum, mute

shtus (der), nonsense

shús-ter (der), shoemaker, cobbler

shvarts, black

sh'-vat, (Heb., *shevat*), fifth month of the Hebrew calendar. The minor festival of *tu b'sh'vat* is celebrated, as the name indicates, on the fifteenth of the month. It marks the beginning of spring in Israel.

shváyg-'n, to keep silent

shvém-lakh (di), mushrooms

shver (der), father-in-law

shver, heavy

shvést-er (di), sister

shvéy-ger-'n (di), sister-in-law

shvíg-'r (di), mother-in-law

shvím-en, to swim

shvínd-'l (der), fraud, swindle

shvits bod (der), steam bath

shvóg-er (der), brother-in-law

shvú-e (di), (Heb., *shvuah*), oath

sí-be (di), cause, reason, explanation

sí-der (der), (Heb., *siddur*), prayer book for weekdays and Sabbaths

sí-men (der), (Heb., *si-man*), sign, omen, token

sím-khe (di), (Heb., *simha*), joy; a happy event

sím-khes tóy-re, (Heb., *simhat torah*), festival of Rejoicing in the Law. Coming immediately after the last day of *sukes* and *sh'mini atseres*, it marks the conclusion of the Torah reading cycle and its immediate recommencement. There is much singing and dancing in the synagogue as seven processions with the Torah scrolls circle the congregation. During the reading of the last portion of Deuteronomy and the first portion of Genesis, young and old alike are called to bless the Torah (See **aliye**). Even young children are accorded the honor in a group. Universally observed although it is not specifically included among the prescribed Biblical festivals.

**sim-pá-tish**, congenial, amenable, sympathetic

**sí-ne (di)**, (Heb., *sinah*), hatred animosity, grudge

**sivan**, See **siv'n**

**sí-v'n**, (Heb., *sivan*), ninth month of the Hebrew calendar. The festival of *shevies*, marking the time when the newly freed Hebrews received the Ten Commandments, is observed on the fifth and sixth of the month.

**skríp-'n**, to squeak

**smé-te-ne (di)**, sweet or sour cream; the elite, upper crust, cream of society; profits off the top

**smí-khe (di)**, (Heb., *semikha*, lit., the laying on of hands), rabbinic ordination. In the time of the sages, a master indicated that a pupil was qualified to serve as rabbi and teacher by placing his hands on the pupil's shoulders. The term has remained, although today, rabbinic seminaries generally graduate students in a group, in the modern academic fashion, and present each student with a rabbinic diploma (also called a *smikhe*) attesting to his qualifications.

**sod (der)**, (Heb., *sod*), secret

**sof**, the weaker version of the 22nd letter of the Hebrew (and Yiddish) letter *tof* ( ת ). The sof is printed and written like the *tof*, but omits the dot, ת, and is pronounced as is the English letter *s*.

**sof (der)**, (Heb., *sof*), end, conclusion

**só-fek (der)**, (Heb., *safek*), doubt

**sort (der)**, type, kind

**sót-'n (der)**, (Heb., *satan*), satan, evil eye

**sóy-kher (der)**, (Heb., *soher*), merchant, seller, tradesman

**sóy-ne (der)**, (Heb., *soneh*), enemy, adversary

**spe-tsi-él**, especially

**spó-dik (der)**, tall fur hat; also, id., head

**staytch**, how come? why, really

**stél-ye (di)**, ceiling

**strá-sh-'n**, to threaten

**strá-sh-'n di genz**, (lit., to threaten the geese); to make an empty threat

**sú-de (di)**, (Heb., *seudah*), festive meal

**sú-kes**, (Heb., *sukkot*), Feast of Tabernacles. One of the three Biblical pilgrimage festivals.  For seven days Jews are commanded to live in small booths or huts (*sukes*), temporary shelters open to the elements, in remembrance of the times when the post-Egypt generation dwelt in tents or other temporary structures during their 40-year sojourn to the Promised Land.  Once settled in Canaan on their allotted lands, Jerusalem (during David's reign) became the capital and the site where his son, Solomon, built the Temple.  By that time, the Jews had become an agrarian people and the thanksgiving aspect of the festival was accentuated.  Coming, as it does, at harvest time, the first fruits of the land and the flock were brought as thanksgiving sacrifices to the Temple by pilgrims from all over the land.  So crowded did Jerusalem become at this season that many were compelled once again to take shelter in temporary huts, which they erected in and around the city.  Today, observant Jews take their meals in the *suke* and spend as much time there each day as possible, even if the festival is marred by rain.

**sukkah,** See **suke**
**sukkos,** See **sukes**
**sukkot,** See **sukes**

# T

**tá-ke,** really

**tákh-lis,** utility, practicality, brass tacks, bottom line

**takh-rí-khim (di),** (Heb., *takhrikhim*), white linen burial shrouds. Judaism holds that death is the great equalizer and that all, rich and poor, should be buried in the same simple two-piece garment, sewn together with long stitches, the threads left unknotted. Regular dress for the deceased is not permitted. Both men and women are clothed in the *takhrikhim* and a head covering. Men are wrapped in their *talis* from which the *tsitsis* have been removed since the dead are not required to observe the commandments.

**tá-lis (der),** (Heb., *talit*), prayer shawl worn by men for morning prayer. Usually white with black or blue horizontal stripes, although it can be of any color. Its most significant features are the *tsitsis*, ritually knotted fringes, bound to each corner in compliance with the Biblical commandment to wear fringes on the corners of garments, so that the wearer may see them and remember his responsibilities to God and man. The *tsitsis* are tied in special knots and windings, which when added together, total 613, the number of positive Biblical commandments.

**tál-mid (der),** (Heb., *talmid*), pupil, disciple

**tál-mid khó-khem (der),** (Heb., *talmid hakham*, disciple of the wise), a Jew learned in scripture

**tál-mid tóy-re,** (Heb., *talmud torah*, lit., the study of the Torah); a school where Torah is taught; religious school

**tál-mud,** (Heb., *talmud*), the voluminous codes of Jewish law representing the collective commentaries and wisdom gathered by thousands of scholars who studied and taught the Law over many centuries, in many lands. It covers a wide variety of subjects: religion, ritual, ethics, liturgy, philosophy, science, medicine, astronomy, astrology, history, geography, commerce, property, criminal and civil law, marriage, festivals, etc. It is also a rich treasure of legends and parables, called *agadah*, which the scholars used in the course of their discussions to make a point or to give an example. There are actually two Talmuds, Babylonian (*talmud bavli*), compiled during the early centuries of the common era and completed in the academies of Babylonia in the 5th century; and the second, the Jerusalem Talmud (*talmud yerushalmi*), completed in the 4th century by Palestinian scholars. The Babylonian Talmud is generally acknowledged as the more authoritative. Both have the same structure; they are based on the Aramaic *gemore* and the Hebrew *mishne*. Over the centuries following the redaction of the Talmud, additional commentaries, opinions and discussions by scholars all over the world were added to the two basic sections and incorporated into the Talmud's pages. These additions are known as *toseftot*. The Talmud is, therefore, the scholastic productivity of Jewish sages and scholars over a period of ten centuries.

**talmud torah**, See **talmid toyre**

**tam (der)**, (Heb., *taam*), taste; also (Heb., *tam*), simpleton

**tá-mez**, (Heb., *tamuz*), tenth month of the Hebrew calendar during which the period marking the beginning of the final days of the besieged Temple in Jerusalem opens on the seventeenth. It is a fast day and known as *shivoser b'tamez*.

**tam gan éy-d'n**, (Heb., *taam gan eden*, lit., the taste of Paradise); delicious!

**tammuz**, See **tomiz**

**ta-nákh**, (Heb., *tanakh*), an acronym representing the three major sections of the Bible: *ta*, for *toyre*, or Pentatench; *na*, for *n'viim*, or Prophets; *kh* for *khetuvim*, writings or wisdom literature.

Pentateuch: Genesis, Exodus, Leviticus, Numbers, Deuteronomy. Prophets: Joshua, Judges, Samuel I, II, Kings I, II, Isaiah, Jeremiah, Ezekiel, Hosea, Joel, Amos, Obadiah, Jonah, Micah, Nahum, Habakuk, Zephaniah, Zechariah, Malachi. Wisdom Literature: Psalms, Proverbs, Job, Song of Songs, Ruth, Lamentations, Ecclesiastes, Esther, Daniel, Ezra-Nehemia, Chronicles.

**tá-nes (der)**, (Heb., *taanit*), fast (abstention from food and drink)

**tán-te (di)**, aunt

**tants (der)**, dance

**tánts-'n**, to dance

**tap-'n**, to paw

**ta-ra-rám (der)**, uproar, commotion, noise

**tá-te (der)**, father

**tá-te-le**, (lit., little father); term of endearment for a boy

**tá-te-nyu**, (lit., dear father); usually, dear Father in Heaven; also, venerable father

**táy-er**, dear, precious, valuable, costly

**táy-er-e**, dear (fem.)

**táy-er-er**, dear (masc.)

**taykh (der)**, river, lake, brook

**táy-ne (di)**, complaint, claim, argument

**taytsh (der)**, translation, explanation

**táy-v'l (der)**, devil

**tég-lakh**, daily

**té-ler (der)**, plate

**tép-'l (dos)**, small pot or cup

**té-rets (der)**, (Heb., *teruts*, answer), alibi, excuse

**tes**, ninth letter of the Hebrew (and Yiddish) alphabet: ט, pronounced as is the letter *t*.

**tevet**, See **teyves**

**tey (di)**, tea

**teyg (dos)**, dough (baking)

**téyg-lakh (di)**, bits of dough baked in honey

**téy-kef**, (Heb., *tekef*), at once, immediately

**teyl (der)**, part, portion

**téyl-'n zikh**, to share, to divide

**téy-ves**, (Heb., *tevet*), fourth month of the Hebrew calendar; a minor fast day, *asarah b'tevet*, falls on the tenth day. It commemorates the day in 586 B.C.E., when the Babylonians began their siege of Jerusalem.

**t'fí-le (di)**, (Heb., *tefilah*), prayer

**t'fí-lin (di)**, (Heb., *tefillin*, lit., prayers), phylacteries, small leather boxes held in place by thin leather thongs which male Jews wear at prayer each weekday morning, along with their *talis*. The boxes contain parchment scrolls on which are inscribed four significant Biblical quotations: section dealing with the dedication of the first born son to the service of God; section commanding the telling and retelling of the story of the Exodus to succeeding generations; section containing the *sh'ma yisrael* which speaks of the unity of God, and the final section, which deals with the Torah's concept of reward and punishment for personal behavior. One box is affixed to the top of the forehead and the other to the upper left arm as commanded in Numbers: "...thou shalt bind them for frontlets between thine eyes and on thine arm..." *t'filin* are not worn on Sabbaths and festivals since these occasions symbolize, in their liturgy and ritual, the concepts of sanctity contained in the parchment scrolls.

**t'fí-se (di)**, (Heb., *tefisah*, lit., holding); jail, prison

**tif**, deep

**tí-lim**, (Heb., *tehilim*), Book of Psalms reputed to have been composed by King David. Many of the 150 psalms constitute an important portion of the daily, Sabbath, and festival liturgies.

**tint (di)**, ink

**tir (di)**, door

**tir tsu tir**, (lit., door to door), next door

**tish (der)**, table

**tisha b'av**, See **tishe bov**

**tísh-e bov**, (Heb., *tisha b'av*), the ninth day of the month of *ov*; fast day commemorating the final fall of the Temple in the year 70.

**tísh-rey,** (Heb., *tishre*), first month of the Hebrew calendar. *rosheshone* falls on the first and second day, *yom kiper* on the tenth, *sukes* on the fifteenth, *shmini atseres* on the 22nd, and *simkhes toyre* on the following day.

**tísh-takh (der),** tablecloth

**tish un náyn-tsik ka-pó-res,** (lit., table and ninety atonement sacrifices); the utmost in uselessness

**t'lí-ye (di),** (Heb., *t'liyah*), gallows

**tnóy-im (di),** (Heb., *t'naim*, conditions), agreement of betrothal entered into by the families of a prospective bride and groom some time prior to the wedding. The contract enumerates such things as dowry, amount of parental support, gifts, housing arrangements, date and place of the wedding, etc.

**tof,** 22nd letter of the Hebrew (and Yiddish) alphabet: ת, pronounced as is the letter *t*.

**tog (der),** day

**tog ayn, tog oys,** day in, day out

**tó-khes (der),** (Heb., *tahat*, below, bottom), buttocks, ass, rump

**tókh-ter (di),** daughter

**tol (der),** valley

**tó-mid,** (Heb., *tamid*), eternal, always, continually

**tó-miz,** (Heb., *tammuz*), tenth month of the Hebrew calendar. A three-week period of mourning for the destruction of the Temple begins on the seventeenth of the month, *shivoser b'tomiz.*

**ton,** to do

**tó-nes (der),** (Heb., *taanit*), fast, abstention from food

**top (der),** pot

**torah,** See **toyre**

**tór-be (di),** sack

**tór-en,** permitted; used mostly in its negative form, *toren nit,* i.e., *yid'n toren nit ess'n tarfes,* Jews are not permitted to eat unclean (ritually) food.

**toyb,** deaf

**toyb (di),** dove

**tóyg-'n,** useful, suitable

**tóyg-'n oyf kapó-res,** (lit., will be useful only as an atonement sacrifice); good for nothing

**tóy-re (di),** (Heb., *torah*, law, teaching), technically, the scroll on which the words of the Pentateuch are inscribed; also refers to the text, itself; in a broader sense denotes the entire range of Jewish knowledge; also id., any knowledge or expertise

**toyt,** dead, death

**tóyt-er (der),** corpse

**tóy-ve (di),** (Heb., *tovah*, goodness), favor, kindness

**tóy-z'nt,** thousand

**trakht (di),** womb

**trákht-'n,** to think

**tref,** See **treyf**

**tréf-'n,** to guess

**trep (di),** steps, stairs

**treyf,** (Heb., *tref*, torn, as by an animal), any food forbidden by Jewish law; also in a broader sense, anything at all forbidden by Jewish law; also id., anything illegal, immoral or improper

**treyst (der),** consolation, solace

**trík-'n,** dry, arid, withered

**trínk-'n,** to drink

**tróg-'n,** to carry, to wear; to be pregnant

**tróm-be-nik (der),** freeloader

**tróp-n (der),** drop; id., whiskey

**tróy-er (der),** grief, sadness, mourning

**tróy-er-ik,** gloomy, sad, melancholy

**tróy-er-'n,** to mourn, to grieve

**troym (der),** dream

**trúk-'n,** dry

**tsá-dik,** eighteenth letter of the Hebrew (and Yiddish) alphabet: צ, pronounced as is the two letter combination, *ts*, as in si*ts*. When a *tsadik* comes as a final letter of a word, it is printed ץ.

**tsá-dik (der),** (Heb., *tsadik*), righteous, pious person; also the title for a distinguished, pious rabbi or scholar

**tsar (der),** sorrow; also czar

**tsar bá-ley khá-yim,** (Heb., *tzaar baaley hayim*; lit., pain to a living creature), Jewish law forbids cruelty to or mistreatment of all living things.

**tsart,** tender, gentle

**tsáts-ke (di),** plaything; shrew, flirt

**tsa-vó-e (di),** (Heb., *tzavaah*), will, testament

**tsáyg-'n,** to show

**tsayt (di),** time, era, epoch

**tsáyt-ung (di),** newspaper

**tse-dó-ke (di),** (Heb., *ts'dakah*), righteousness, justice; most often used to mean charity.

**tse-dréyt,** mixed-up, confused, unbalanced

**tse-káy-en,** to chew; to consider, to think about

**tse-kríg-'n zikh,** to quarrel

**tse-krókh-'n,** unkempt, unappetizing, uncoordinated, creaky

**tsen,** ten

**tse-shnáyd-'n,** to cut up

**tse-shóy-bert,** unkempt, uncombed

**tse-téyl-'n,** to divide

**tse-tráyb-'n,** to disperse, to dispell

**tséyl-'n,** to count

**tséyl-n s'fí-re,** to ritually count the days between *peysakh* and *shevies* in commemoration of ancient gift offerings brought to the Temple during that period.

**t'shatshke,** See **tsatske**

**tsháy-nik (der),** teapot

**tshép-'n,** to touch, to molest, to pester, to disturb, to annoy

**tshó-lent (der),** Sabbath dish of potatos, meat, and beans, cooked before the onset of the Sabbath and kept warm in a prelit oven in compliance with the prohibition against cooking on the Sabbath.

**tsí-be-le (di),** onion

**tsi-gáy-ner (der),** gypsy

**tsí-mer (der),** room

**tsí-mes (der),** dessert, usually a stew of carrots, prunes, and other fruits; served as a side dish with Sabbath or festive meals; also fuss, commotion, big deal, i.e., Don't make such a big *tsimes* over it.

**tsí-rung (di),** jewelry

**tsí-ter-'n (dos),** chills

**tsí-ter-'n,** to tremble

**tsí-tses (di),** (Heb., *tsitsit*, fringes) Ritual fringes worn by male Jews who are commanded to affix them to the corners of their garments as a constant reminder of the responsibility to love the Lord and to live according to His law. In modern times, these fringes are no longer placed on outer garments. They are to be found instead, on each corner of the *talis* (prayer shawl), and on small garments worn under the shirt by particularly observant Jews (See **arbe kanfes**). Since the law commands the Jew that he shall see the *tsitses*, the fringes on these small undergarments are allowed to hang out from the shirt. *tsitses* are not ordinary fringes, but are tied in a prescribed fashion with windings and knots which equal 613 in number, the number of positive commandments in the Bible.

**tsíts-ke (di),** breast, tit

**tsíy-en,** to pull, to draw, to extend

**tsóf'n,** (Heb., *tsafon*), north

**tsól-'n,** to pay

**tson (der),** tooth
**tson dók-ter (der),** dentist
**tsó-re (di),** (Heb.; *tzarah*), trouble, affliction, woe
**tsorn (der),** anger, fury
**tsu,** to, too much
**tsu ál-de shvárts-e ríkh-es,** (lit., to all the black furies).  To hell, drop dead.
**tsu-dréyt,** insane
**tsú-fal (der),** accident
**tsu-fríd-'n,** satisfied
**tsú-gan-ven-en,** to steal, to make off with
**tsu ge-zúnt,** (lit., to health).  God bless you; the response to a sneeze.
**tsú-ker (der),** sugar
**tsu-kér-ke (di),** candy
**tsu-kér-ni-ye (di),** candystore
**tsú-kunft (der),** future
**tsu-létst,** final
**tsu-líb,** for, because of, for the sake of
**tsú-makh-'n,** to close
**tsú-makh-'n an oyg,** (lit., to close an eye), to sleep; to die
**tsum báy-shpil,** for example
**tsu-mísh-'n,** to confuse, complicate, to mix up
**tsung (di),** tongue
**tsu-rík,** back, return
**tsú-shtel-en,** deliver, cater, provide
**tsú-troy (der),** faith
**tsú-tsik (der),** colt, young person, "eager beaver"
**tsu-zá-men,** together
**tsvang (di),** pliers
**tsván-tsik,** twenty
**tsvey,** two
**tsvéy-te (di),** second (ordinal)
**tsvok (der),** nail (in construction)
**tukh (di),** dustcloth, washcloth
**tú-m'l (der),** noise, confusion, excitement
**tún-k'l,** dark, dim
**túr-me (di),** prison

# U

ú-ger-ke (di), cucumber
ú-me-tik, sad
ú-met-i-kayt, gloom, sadness
ú-me-tum, everywhere
um-ge-lúmp-ert, clumsy, awkward, uncoordinated
úm-glik (der), disaster, tragedy, misfortune
úm-ker-'n, to return, to turn around
úm-kum-en, to perish
um-még-likh, impossible
um-shúld-ig, innocent
um-zíst, in vain, free of charge
undz, us, to us
u-ni-ver-si-tét (der), university
ún-ter, under, beneath
un-ter-drík-'n, to oppress, to subjugate
ún-ter-gan-ven-en zíkh, to sneak up on
ún-ter-geb-'n zikh, to surrender
ún-ter-gey-en, to sink, to fail, to founder
ún-ter-her-'n, to overhear, to eavesdrop
ún-ter-kóyf-'n, to bribe
ún-ter-shtel-en a fís-'l, (lit., to put a foot under one); trip someone, to subvert
ún-tersh-te shú-re (di), bottom line, total, net price
ún-ter-vaks-'n, to grow up unnoticed
ún-ter-varf-'n, to abandon, to plant something on someone
ún-ter-vesh (dos), underclothes
úr-tel (der), verdict, decision
úr-zakh (der), reason, cause

# V

va-gí-ne (di), vagina
va-ká-tsi-ye (di), vacation
vald (der), forest, woods
vá-len (di), elections
vál-ger-'n, (lit., to roll); to roam aimlessly, to bum around
vá-ne (di), bath, bathtub
vant (di), wall
vants (der), bedbug
vá-rem, warm, cordial
va-rúm, why
várt-'n, to wait
várts-froy (di), midwife
vá-ser (dos), water
vásh-'n, to wash
vav, sixth letter of the Hebrew (and Yiddish) alphabet: ו , pronounced as is the
   letter *v*.
vayb (di), wife
váyn-sh'l (der), cherry
váyn-troyb (di), grape
vays, white
vayt, far
váy-zer (der), clock hand, pointer
váyz-'n, to show, to display
vék-er (der), alarm clock
véks-'l (dos), note, IOU
vél-en, to want, to desire, to wish
vél-kher, which
vélt-likh, worldly, secular
vém-en, whom
ven, when
ven nor, whenever
ver, who
vért-er (di), words
vért-ful, valuable
vesh (dos), laundry (things to be washed)
véy-d'l (der), tail

82

**veykh,** soft, tender
**véyn-en,** to cry
**véy-nik,** insufficient
**véy-nik-er,** less
**véy-tik (der),** pain
**veyts (der),** wheat
**vi a-zóy,** how
**ví-der,** again
**ví-der kol,** echo
**vi-fíl,** how much?, how many
**vi-fíl iz der zéy-ger,** what time is it
**vi halt es mit aykh,** how are you
**vi in vá-ser a-ráyn,** (lit., as though fallen into the sea); to disappear without a trace
**víkht-ik,** important
**vi kumt es,** how come
**vi lang,** how long
**vild,** wild
**vínt-er (der),** winter
**vínt-'l (dos),** breeze
**ví-s'n-shaft (di),** knowledge, science
**ví-s'n-shaft-ler (der),** scientist
**vits (der),** joke
**vi vayt,** how far
**ví-yes (di),** eyelashes
**vóg-'n (der),** wagon
**vókh-e-dik,** commonplace, everyday
**vón-tse (di),** moustache
**vort (dos),** word, promise
**vóyn-en,** to reside
**vóyn-ung (di),** residence
**vu,** where
**vún-der (der),** wonder, miracle
**vún-der-n,** to wonder
**vu-nór,** wherever
**vus gíkh-er,** as soon as possible
**vus tut zikh,** what's up

# Y

**yákh-ne (di),** shrew, busybody, haggler, loudmouth

**yam (der),** (Heb., *yam*), sea

**yá-nu-ar,** January

**yár-mil-ke (di),** skullcap

**yarmulke,** See **yarmilke**

**yá-sh'r kóy-akh,** (Heb., *yiasher kokhakha*, lit., more power to you); traditional congratulations on a deed well done; particularly for participation in a ritual act.

**yé-der,** each, every

**yé-ke (der),** a German Jew; punctiliously correct. First became popular in the early 20th century in Palestine when the German emigrants insisted on wearing their traditional formal attire, in spite of a climate and sociological atmosphere which called for less formal clothes. It is derived from the German word for jacket.

**yén-te (di),** feminine name; also busybody, gossip, nosy person. Gained its negative connotations from a very popular character, *yente telebende*, the protagonist in a widely read humor column written by the Yiddish humorist, B. Kovner, in the *Jewish Daily Forward* in the 1920s and 1930s.

**ye-rú-she (di),** inheritance, legacy

**ye-ru-sho-lá-yim,** Jerusalem

**ye-shí-ve (di),** (Heb., *yeshivah*, sitting, academy), a school of intensive Jewish study where Talmud, law, and ritual are the major subjects. The *yeshive* ranges in size and prestige, from a simple table in the *bes medresh* of a synagogue to a modern institution serving hundreds of students. During the European experience most were of the simple type, although there were a good number of large, formal institutions in the larger cities. Male students only were trained in *yeshives*. Today, both male and female students study in *yeshives*, although the more orthodox schools have separate facilities for boys and girls.

**ye-shí-ve bókh-'r (der),** male *yeshive* student

**ye-sú-rim (di),** (Heb., *yesurim*), troubles

**yéy-tser hó-re (der),** (Heb., *yetzer hara*), evil inclination; erotic yearning, lust

**yéy-tser tov (der),** (Heb., *yetzer hatov*), inclination to do good, to be pious

**yid (der),** Jew

**yíd-e-ne (di),** Jewess

**yí-dish,** Yiddish

yíd-ish-kayt (dos), Judaism, Jewishness

yí-khes (der), (Heb., *yihus*, genealogical pedigree), privilege, status by virtue of family station, scholarship, wealth

yi-mákh sh-móy, (Heb., *yimakh sh'mo*), may his name be blotted out; a particularly strong malediction, not spoken lightly.

yíng-'l (dos), lad

yí-shuv (der), (Heb., *yishuv*, settlement), out of the way hamlet or tiny village

yi-shúv-nik (der), small town resident

yis-ról, (Heb., *yisrael*), Jew; a Jew who is neither a *koyn* or *leyvi*, the majority of the congregation of Israel (See koyn, leyvi)

yíz-k'r, (Heb., *yizkor*, may (God) remember), opening word of memorial prayer recited in the synagogue on *yom kiper, sukes, peysakh, shevies.*

yó-ge-nish (dos), rush

yold (der), fool, simpleton, half-wit

yom kí-per, (Heb., *yom kippur*), Day of Atonement. The concluding holy day of the most sacred season of the Jewish religious calendar, which begins with *rosheshone*, New Year. This is followed by an interval of penitential days and capped on the tenth day, by the fast day of *yom kiper*. It is a day of deep soul searching, prayer, penitence, and complete abstinence from food and drink for 24 hours.

yom kippur, See yom kiper

yón-tev (der), (Heb., *yom tov*), holiday

yón-tev-dik, festive, holiday mood

yor-hún-dert (der), century

yór-tsayt (der), anniversary of death. Jews observe a full 24-hour period of mourning on the anniversary of the death of a parent, child, mate, sibling. A memorial candle is lit, the mourner attends the synagogue for the three services of the day during which he recites the Kaddish (doxology). (See kadish).

yoykh, rich fatty broth, chicken soup

yóy-resh (der), (Heb., *yoresh*), heir

yóy-sher (der), (Heb., *yosher*), justice, morality, fairness

yud, tenth letter of the Hebrew (and Yiddish) alphabet: ' , pronounced as is the letter *y* and *i* in the words *yet* and *bid.*

yúng-er (der), young one

# Z

zaft (der), juice
záft-ik, juicy, luscious, well endowed, overweight
zak (der), sack
zal (der), auditorium
zalts (di), salt
zamd (dos), sand
zám'l-en, to collect, to gather
za-pás (der), stock, supply
zat, sated
zay a-zóy gut, (lit., be so good), please
zá-yin, seventh letter of the Hebrew (and Yiddish) alphabet: ז , pronounced
   as is the letter z.
zayn, to be
zayt, since
zayt (di), side
ze-khí-ye (di), (Heb., z'khut), privilege
zékh-ts'n, sixteen
zékh-tsik, sixty
zeks, six
zélt-'n, seldom
zém-er (der), (Heb., zemer), song
zen, to see
zets (der), blow, punch, slap
zey, they
zéy-de (der), grandfather
zéy-en, to see
zéy-er, their
zéy-ger (der), clock, watch
zéy-ger-makh-er (der), watchmaker
zhe, suffix following a verb in the imperative, meaning, so . . . ; i.e., kum-zhe, so,
   come; zay-zhe ge-zúnt, so, be well
zhlob (der), clod, boor, oaf
zhur-na-líst (der), journalist
zi, she
zí-bi-tsik, seventy
zíb-i-ts'n, seventeen

**zíb-'n,** seven
**zid-ler-áy (dos),** scolding
**zíd-'n,** to boil
**zifts (der),** sigh
**zikh,** one's self
**zíkh-er,** surely, confident, deft, secure, certain
**zikh shlóg-'n al khet,** (lit., to beat one's breast as in the recital of the atonement prayer of *al khet*, a long list of sins in the *yom kiper* liturgy, each of which is introduced by *al khet*, "For the sin which we have committed"; regret, repentance, pangs of conscience, self condemnation, to reproach oneself
**zi-kór-'n (der),** (Heb., *zikaron*), memory, recollection
**zíl-ber (dos),** silver
**zínd (di),** sin
**zíng-en,** to sing
**zínk-'n,** to sink
**zis,** sweet
**zís-kayt,** sweetness, sweetie
**zíts-'n,** to sit
**zíts-ung (di),** meeting (organizational)
**zí-vig (der),** (Heb., *zivug*, pair), predestined partner in marriage. A folk myth has it that God chooses one's partner in marriage 40 days before he or she is born.
**z'-khús (der),** (Heb., *z'khut*), merit, special privilege; earned merit one accumulates for the world to come.
**z'mí-res (di),** (Heb., *zemirot*, songs), hymns and religious songs sung around the Sabbath or festival table
**zóg-'n,** to say
**zók-'n (der),** (Heb., *zaken*), old man
**zók-n (di),** socks, stockings
**zol mayns í-ber-geyn,** (lit., let mine go by), I forgive, let it pass
**zol zayn a-zóy,** (lit., so be it), have it your way, thats the deal
**zóy-er,** sour
**zóy-e-re ú-ger-ke,** sour pickle
**zúkh-'n,** to look for
**zú-mer (der),** summer
**zun (di),** sun
**zun (der),** son
**zún-en shayn (di),** sunshine
**zún-tik,** Sunday
**zup (di),** soup, sip

# A

abandoned, pust
abandoned wife, a-gú-ne (di)
(to) abandon secretly, uń-ter-varf-'n
abdomen, boykh (der)
about, a-rúm
absent, ni-tó
absolutely, a-vá-de
(to) accept, ón-nem-en
(to) accept another's good fortune, far-gín-en
accident, tśu-fal (der)
according to, loyt
account, khésh-b'n (der), rékh-e-nung (der)
acculturated immigrants, géy-le (di)
(to) act (on stage), shpíl-en
act, shtik (der)
(to) accuse, ba-shúl-dig-'n
acquaintance (fem.), ba-kán-te (di)
acquaintance (masc.), ba-kán-ter (der)
(to become) acquainted with, ba-kén-en zikh
active, rír-ev-dig
actor, ak-ti-yór (der)
actress, ak-te-rí-se (di)
Adam, ó-dom
(to) add (process), ré-khen-en
address (speech), ré-de (di)
address (house number, street, etc.), a-drés (der)
(to) admire, gláykh-'n, ba-vún-der-'n
adult, ful-kóm, der-váks-'n
adultery, ní-ef (der)
adversary, sóy-ne (der), kon-ku-rént (der)
advice, éy-tse (di)
advisable, k'-dáy
affliction, ón-shik-e-nesh (dos), tsó-re (di)
afire, es brent
afternoon, nokh-mí-tog
again, noch a mol, ví-der

**against,** ké-g'n
**(to) aggravate,** der-géy-en di yór-'n
**agile,** rír-ev-dig
**(to) agree,** más-kim zayn
**ague,** ka-dó-khes (dos)
**aha,** ot
**air,** luft (die)
**alarm clock,** vék-er (der)
**alibi,** té-rets (der)
**alien,** in der fremd, frémd-er (der)
**alive,** lé-be-dik
**all,** alts, á-le
**all in one piece,** b'shó-lem
**(to) allow,** lóz-'n, der-lóyb-'n
**all right,** me-khe-téy-se
**almonds,** mándl-'n (di)
**almost,** koym, ot-ot, k-'mát
**alone,** a-léyn
**aloud,** óyf-'n kol, hoykh
**alphabet,** á-lef beys (der)
**also,** oykh
**alternative,** bréy-re (di)
**although,** dokh, khotsh
**always,** tó-mid, á-le mol
**am,** bin
**amen,** ó-meyn
**amenable,** sim-pá-tish
**amulet,** ka-méy-e (di)
**(to) amuse,** a-muz-ír-'n
**amusement,** far-váyl-ung (di)
**angel,** má-lakh (der)
**Angel of Death,** má-lakh-a-mó-ves (der)
**anger,** tsorn (der), kas (der)
**angry,** beyz, broy-gez, in kas, ón-ge-tsoy-g'n
**animosity,** sí-ne (di)
**ankle,** knékh-k'l (dos)
**(to) annoy,** díl-'n a kop, der-gey-en di yór-'n, tshép-'n
**another,** án-der-er
**(to) annul,** bót-'l mákh-'n
**answer,** ént-fer (der)

**(to) anticipate,** ríkh-t'n zíkh
**anything at all,** abí vus
**anything goes,** héf-ker pét-rish-ke
**anyway,** b'méy-le, say vi say
**anywhere,** vu nor
**apostate,** me-shú-med (der)
**apparently,** klóy-mersht
**(to) appear as,** óys-zey-en
**(to) appear in a dream,** kú-men tsu khó-lem
**(to) appear like,** hób-n a pó-nim
**(to) applaud,** pátsh-'n
**apple,** é-p'l (der)
**applesauce,** é-p'l tsí-mes
**appropriate,** pás-ik
**appropriately,** bal-e-bá-tish
**approximately,** k-'mát, bi-é-rekh
**April,** a-príl
**apron,** fár-takh (der)
**are,** bist
**(to) argue,** óys-tayn-en zikh
**argument,** táy-ne (di)
**arid,** trik-'n
**(to) arise,** óyf-shtey-en
**arithmetic,** a-rit-mé-tik (di)-mé
**arm (anat.),** ár-em (der)
**aroma,** réy-akh (der), a-ro-mát (der)
**(to) arrest,** a-rest-ír-'n
**(to) arrive,** ón-kum-en, kúm-en
**(to) arrive at the wrong place,** far-fór-'n
**arrogance,** gáy-ve (di), khúts-pe (di)
**arrogant person,** á-zes pó-nim (der)
**art,** kunst (di)
**as (at the same point in time),** b'eys
**(to be) ashamed,** shé-men zikh
**ashen,** bleykh
**ash tray,** ásh-tets'l (dos)
**as if,** klóy-mersht
**(to) ask,** frég-'n
**ass,** tó-khes (der), hínt-'n (der)
**ass (donkey),** éy-z'l (der)

asset, máy-le (di)
assets, far-méy-g'n
assignment, lék-tsi-ye (di), óyf-ga-be (di)
assistance, hilf (di)
as soon as possible, vus gí-kher
at least, khotsh
at once, téy-kef
atonement ritual, ka-pó-res
(to) attack, ba-fál-'n
attic, bóy-dem (der)
audience, óy-lem (der)
audition, pró-be (di)
(to) audition, óys-her-'n, géb-'n pró-be
auditorium, zal (der)
August, óy-gust
aunt, tán-te (di), míme (di)
author, me-khá-b'r (der), shráyb-er (der)
auto, ma-shín (di)
automaton, góy-lem (der)
autumn, herbst (der)
(to) avert, óys-mayd-'n
(to) avoid, óys-mayd-'n
awake, of
(to) awaken, óyf-khap-'n zikh, óyf-shtey-en
away, a-vék
awkward, um-ge-lúmp-ert
axe, hak (di)

# B

bachelor, bókh-er (der)
bachelor (*confirmed*), ált-er bó-kher (der)
back (upper region; anat.), pléy-tse (di)
back, (*return*), tsu-rík
back and forth, a-hín un k'rik
bad, shlekht
bad luck, shle-má-z'l (der)
bag of troubles, pék-'l tsó-res (dos)
(to) bake, bák-'n
baker, bék-er (der)
bakery, be-ker-áy (di)
baldpate, plikh (der)
banana, ba-nán (der)
bank, bank (di)
banker, bank-ír (der)
bankrupt, me-khú-le
barefoot, bór-ves
bargain, bí-lik, bí-lik vi borsht, me-tsí-e (di)
Bar Mitsvah, bar míts-ve (der)
barrage, shi-se-ráy (dos)
barrel, fés-'l (dos)
bashful, shém-ev-dik
bastard, mám-z'r (der)
bath, vá-ne (di)
(to) bathe one's self, bód-'n zikh
bathtub, vá-ne (di)
Bat Mitsvah, bas míts-ve (di)
(to) be, zayn
(to) be able, kén-en
beadle, shá-mes (der)
beam (wooden), klotz (der)
bean, bé-b'l (dos)
beans, ár-bes (der, di), bé-b'l (dos), béb-lakh (di)
(to) bear, oyś-halt-'n
beard, bord (di)
beard (short, Van Dyke), berd'l (dos)

beast, khá-ye (di)
beautiful person, shéyn-kayt (di)
beauty, shéyn-kayt (di)
because of, tsu-líb
bed, bet (di), ge-léyg-er (dos)
bedbug, vants (di)
bedding, bét-ge-vant (dos)
bedroom, shlóf-tsim- er (der)
bed sheet, láy-lakh (der)
beets, bú-ri-kes (di)
beet soup, borsht (der)
before, éy-der
before one's time, far der tsayt
beggar, shlép-er (der), shnór-er (der)
(to) begin, ón-fang-en
(to) begrudge, nit far-gín-en
behind, hín-t'n (der)
(to) be in need of, féyl-n
(to) be late, far-shpét-ik-'n
belch, grepts (der)
(to) believe, glóyb-'n
belly-boykh (der)
bellyache, bóykh-vey-tik (der)
(to) belong to, ge-hér-'n
beloved, lib
below, a-rún-ter
belt, gart'l (dos)
(to) be missing, féyl-n
bench, bank (di)
(to) bend one's ear, hák'n a tcháy-nik
beneath, ún-ter
benediction, brókh-e (di)
bereaved one, ó-v'l (der)
bereavement, a-véy-les (dos)
beset by hard luck, oyf ge-hók-te tsó-res
(to) be short of, féyl-'n
beside, léb-'n
be still, sha
betrothal contract, tnóy-im (di)
betrothed, far-knást

**betrothed (boy)**, khó-s'n (der)
**betrothed (girl)**, ká-le (di)
**better**, bé-ser
**Bible commentary**, mish-ne (di), ge-mó-re (di)
**big shot**, knák-er (der), mákh-er (der)
**bill**, khésh-b'n (der)
**bird**, fóy-g'l (der)
**birdie**, féy-ge-le (dos)
**bit**, píts-'l (dos)
**(to) bite**, báys-'n
**bizzare**, me-shú-ge
**(to) blabber**, pláp-len
**black**, shvarts
**black of night**, khóy-shekh (der)
**blame**, shuld (di)
**bland**, pá-re-ve, on zalts un on fé-fer
**blanket**, kól-di-re (di)
**(to) bless**, béntsh-'n
**blessing for deliverance**, béntsh-'n góy-m'l
**blessing the Sabbath lights**, likht béntsh-'n
**blessing over bread**, móy-tse
**blessing over wine**, kí-dish
**blind**, blind
**blood**, blut (dos)
**blood vessels**, ó-der-'n (di)
**(to) bloom**, blíy-en
**(to) blossom**, blíy-en
**(to) blow**, blóz-'n
**blow**, má-ke (di), khmál-ye (der), zets (der), shos (der)
**blue**, bloy (color); ú-me-tik (sad)
**(to) boast**, blóz-'n fun zikh, ba-rím-en zikh
**body**, kér-per (der)
**boil**, má-ke (di)
**(to) boil**, zíd-'n
**bolt**, shroyf (der)
**bone**, beyn (der)
**book (sacred)**. séy-fer (der)
**book (secular)**, bukh (der)
**boor**, zhlob (der), pots (der), shmok (der)
**boots**, shtív-'l (di)

border (geogr.), gré-nets (di)
bore, núd-nik (der)
born, ge-bóy-r'n
born loser, shle-má-z'l (der)
boss, ba-le-bós (der)
both, béy-de
(to) bother, núdg-'n, mú-tsh-'n
bottom line, tákh-lis (der)
bow tie, shnips (der)
box, kást-'n (der)
brains (anat.), gír-'n (di)
brains, séy-kh'l (der)
brand new, shpó-g'l nay
brass tacks, tákh-lis
bread, broyt (dos)
breadwinner, far-dín-er (der)
breakfast, í-ber-bay-s'n (dos)
(to) break off, í-ber-rays-'n
breast, brust (di), tsíts-ke (di)
breath, luft (die), ó-tem (der)
(to) breathe, ó-tem-en
bribe, kha-bár (der)
(to) bribe, ún-ter-koyf-'n
bride, ká-le (di)
(to) bring, bréng-en
broken, mé-khú-le
broken down, kál-ye
broker, mék-ler (der)
brook, taykh (der)
broth, yoykh (di)
brothel, háy-z'l (dos)
brother, brú-der (der)
brother-in-law, shvó-ger (der)
brown, broyn
buckwheat groats, ká-she (di)
buddy, gú-ter brí-der (der)
(to) build, bóy-en
building, bín-y'n (der)
bulb (electric), lémp-'l (dos)
bullet, koyl (di)

**bull in a china shop,** vi a yóv-'n in sú-ke
**bum,** shlép-er (der)
**bump,** hóts-ke (di)
**bunch,** khév-re (di), é bán-de (di)
**buried (state of being),** ba-grób-'n
**(to) burn,** brén-en
**(to) burst,** pláts-'n
**business,** hánd-'l (der)
**business,** ge-shéft (dos)
**busy,** far-nú-men
**busybody,** kókh-lef-'l (dos), yákh-ne (di)
**but,** ó-ber
**butcher,** kó-tsef (der)
**butcher block,** klots (der)
**(to) butt in,** a-ráyn-mish-'n
**buttocks,** tó-khes (der), hín-t'n (der)
**buyer,** kóy-ne (der)

# C

cabbage, kroyt (dos)
cabinet, shá-fe (di), or'n (der), kás-t'n (der)
cage, shtayg (di)
cake, lé-kakh (der)
calendar, lú-akh (der)
calm, rú-ig
camera, a-pa-rát (der)
camp (military, penal, concentration), lág-er (der)
candelabrum (for ritual use), me-nóy-re (di)
candlestick, láyḱht-er (der)
candy, tsu-kér-ke (di)
candy store, tsu-kér-ni-ye (di)
cantor, khá-z'n
cantor's wife, khá-z'n-te (di)
capable, féy-ig, óys-toyg-n
cape, mán-t'l (der)
car, ma-shín (di)
carefree, on zórg-'n
careful, óp-ge-hit
caress, glet (der)
carraway seeds, kim'l (der)
carrot, mer (der)
(to) carry, tróg-'n
cart in front of the horse, móy-she ka-póyr
cash, me-zú-men (dos)
(to) cast a pall, far-shtér-'n
cat, kats (di)
(to) catch, kháp-'n
(to) catch one's breath, óp-khap-'n dem ó-tem
(to) catch red-handed, kháp-'n bay der hant
(to) cater, tsú-shtél-'n
cat-o'-nine-tails, kán-tshik (der)
cause, sí-be (di)
cavity, lokh (der)
ceiling, stél-ye (di)
celery, se-le-rí-ye (di)

cellar, kél-er (der)
cemetery, bes-óy-lom (der)
center, mít-'n (der)
century, yor-hún-dert (der)
cereal, ká-she (di)
certain, zí-kher
certainly, a-vá-de
chain, keyt (di)
chance, ge-lé-gen-hayt (di)
(to) change one's mind, kha-ró-te hób-n
chaos, hék-dish (der)
chap, bókh-er (der)
(to) charge, rékh-en-en
charity, tse-dó-ke (di)
charity case, me-ká-b'l (der)
cheap, bí-lik, ge-méyn, níd-rik
cheap garment, shmá-te (di)
cheap stuff, kha-zer-áy (dos)
check (restaurant), khésh-b'n (der)
cheek (anat.), bak (di)
cheese, kez (der)
chef (masc.), ké-kher (der)
chef (fem.), kékh-ne (di)
chemistry, khém-i-ye (di)
cherry (sour), váyn-sh'l (der)
cherry (sweet), karsh (di)
chest (wood), ór-'n (der), kás-t'n (der)
(to) chew, ká-yen, tse-káy-en
chicken fat, shmalts (der)
chicken soup, yoykh (di)
child, kind (dos)
childhood, kínd-er yór-'n (di)
chills, tsí-ter'n (dos)
chimney, kóym-en (der)
chin, kin (di)
choice, bréy-re (di)
cholera, kho-lé-ri-ye (di)
(to) choose, oýs-klayb-'n
Christian, krist (der)
church, kloýs-ter (der)

**cigarette**, pa-pi-rós (der)
**circle**, rud (der)
**circumcision (ritual)**, bris (der)
**(to) circumcise**, má-le zayn
**citron**, és-rig (der)
**city**, shtot (di)
**claim**, táy-ne (di)
**class**, klas (der)
**clean**, reyn
**cleanliness**, reýn-kayt (di)
**clear**, klor
**cleaver**, hak-mé-ser (der)
**clergy**, kley kóy-desh (di)
**clever**, klug
**clock**, zéy-ger (der)
**clock hand**, váy-zer (der)
**clod**, zhlob (der)
**(to) close**, far-mákh-'n
**closed**, ge-shlós-'n
**closet**, shá-fe (di)
**cloth (dusting, cleaning)**, tukh (di)
**clothing**, kléyd-ung (di)
**cloud**, khmár-e (di)
**clown**, pa-yátz (der)
**clumsy**, um-ge-lúmp-ert
**clumsy oaf**, zhlob (der)
**clumsy one**, kál-yi-ke (der), klots (der)
**coarse**, grob
**coarse fellow**, grób-'r yung (der)
**coarse person**, bal-e-gó-le (der)
**coat (long gabardine)**, ka-pó-te (di)
**cobbler**, shús-ter (der)
**cock**, hon (der)
**coffee**, ká-ve (di)
**coffin**, kást-'n (der), ó-r'n (der)
**coin**, mat-béy-e (di)
**cold**, kalt, kelt (di)
**cold (common cold)**, far-kí-lung (di)
**collar**, kól-ner (der)
**(to) collect**, zám'l-en

**collection box,** púsh-ke (di)
**color,** ko-lír (der), farb (di)
**colt,** tsú-tsik (der)
**comb,** kém-'l (dos)
**(to) come to one's senses,** kúm-en óyf-'n séy-kh'l
**come to terms,** dúrkh-ku-men
**comfortable,** be-kvém
**comforter,** kól-di-re (di)
**comic,** lets (der), kó-mi-ker (der)
**command,** ba-fél (der)
**commandment,** ge-bót (dos), míts-ve (di)
**commerce,** hánd-'l (der)
**(to) commit suicide,** ón-ton zikh a máy-se, ba-géy-en zélbst-mord
**common,** gé-meyn, prost
**commonplace,** vókh-e-dig
**common sense,** séy-kh'l (der)
**commotion,** tsí-mes (der)
**communal leader (fem.),** gá-bi-te (di)
**communist,** róyt-er (der), kom-u-níst (der)
**community,** ke-hí-le (di)
**company (business),** fír-me (di); **(social),** gest (di)
**(to) compare,** far-gláykh-'n
**compassion,** rakh-mó-nes
**compatriot,** lánds-man (der)
**compendium of Jewish laws,** shúl-kh'n ó-rekh (der)
**competitor,** kon-ku-rént (der)
**complainer,** kvetsh (der)
**(to) complain loudly,** kvítsh-'n
**complaint,** táy-ne (di)
**complete,** gants, ful-kóm
**completely,** in gánts-'n
**(to) complicate,** tsu-mísh-'n
**(to) conceal,** be-hált-'n
**conceit,** gáy-ve (di)
**conceited,** ón-ge-bloz-'n
**concern,** dáy-ge (di)
**conditions (legal),** ba-díng-ung-en (di)
**conference,** ba-rát-ung (di)
**confidence,** bi-tókh-'n
**confident,** zíkh-er

(to) confuse, tsu-mísh-'n
confused, tse-dréyt
(to be) confused, a-rúm-géy-en on a kop
confusion, tú-m'l (der), mísh-mash (der)
congenial, sim-pá-tish
(to) congratulate, óp-geb-'n maz'l tov
congratulations, yá-sh'r kóy-akh
congregation, ke-hí-le (di)
connoisseur, méy-vin (der)
(to) consent, más-kim zayn
(to) consider, klér-'n, tse-káy-en
consolation, ne-khó-me (di), treyst (der)
(to) contemplate, klér-'n
continually, tó-mid
contraption, makh-er-áy-ke (di)
conversation, shmus (der)
(to) convert from Judaism, shmád-'n zikh
(to) convince, áyn-red-'n
convulsions, ka-dó-khes (dos)
cook (masc.), ké-kher (der)
cook (fem.), ké-kher-'n (di)
(to) cook, kókh-'n
cookie, kíkh-'l (dos)
cool, kil
(to) copulate, pór-'n zikh
cordial, vá-rem
cork, kó-rik (der)
corpse, mes (der), tóyt-er (der)
correct, ríkht-ik, ge-rékht
costly, táy-er
cough, hust (der)
(to) cough constantly, ún-ter-hust-'n
(to) count, tséyl-'n
(to) count out, óys-tseyl-en
countryman, lánds-man (der)
courage, ge-vú-re (di), mut (der)
court (legal), ge-ríkht (dos)
court (structural, royal), hoyf (der)
courteous, éy-d'l

**courtyard**, hoyf (der)
**cousin (masc.)**, ku-zín (der)
**cousin (fem.)**, ku-zín (der)
**cow**, ku (di)
**cow dung**, búb-ke (di)
**(to be) coy**, lóz-'n zikh bét-'n
**cracklings**, grí-vi-nes (di)
**craft**, fakh (der)
**craftsman**, bal me-ló-khe (der)
**cramp**, kramf (der)
**crate**, kást-'n (der)
**(to) crawl**, kríkh-'n
**crazy**, me-shú-ge
**creaky**, tse-shóy-bert
**cream (sweet or sour)**, smé-te-ne (di)
**cream cheese**, shmír-kez (der)
**cream of the crop**, éy-bersht-e fun shtéy-s'l (dos)
**crease**, kneytsh (der)
**Creator**, ba-shé-fer (der)
**crepe**, blín-tse (di)
**cripple**, kál-yi-ke (der)
**cripple (lame)**, krúm-er (der)
**critical situation**, shmol hált-'n, krí-tish
**crooked**, krum
**crowd**, óy-lem (der)
**crude person**, klots (der)
**crux**, í-ker (der)
**(to) cry**, véyn-en
**(to) cry out**, shráy-en, ge-váld-e-v'n
**cucumber**, ú-ger-ke (di)
**cure**, re-fú-e (di)
**(to) curse**, shélt-'n
**cushion**, kísh-'n (der), **(small)** kí-she-le (dos)
**customer**, kóy-ne (der)
**(to) cut**, shnáyd-'n
**(to) cut (with scissors)**, óp-sher-'n
**cutlet**, kot-lét (der)
**(to) cut up**, tse-shnáyd-'n
**czar**, tsar (der)

# D

daily, tég-lakh
dairy foods, míl-khik
damage, shód-'n (der)
(to) dance, tánts-'n
danger, sa-kó-ne (di), ge-fár (der)
dangerous, ge-fér-lakh
dark, fín-ster, tún-k'l
darkness, khóy-shekh (der)
darling, bú-be-le, táy-e-re
date (calendar), dá-te (di)
date, fayg (di)
daughter, tókh-ter (di)
day, tog (der)
day in, day out, tog ayn, tog oys
Day of Atonement, yom kí-per
dead, toyt
(the) dead, méy-sim (di), tóyt-e (di)
deaf, toyb
(to) deal, hándl-en
dear (costly), táy-er
dear, lib, táy-er
dear God, gót-en-yu
death, toyt (der)
death anniversary, yór-tsayt
(to) debate, óys-tay-nen zikh, de-ba-tír-'n
debt, khoyv (der)
decayed (foods or other organic matter), far-fóylt
(to) deceive, óp-nar-'n
December, de-tsém-ber
decent, áyn-shten-dig, láy-tish, fayn
decently, bal-e-bá-tish
(to) decide, ba-shlís-'n, ba-shtím-en
decided, ba-shtímt, ba-shlós-'n
decision, úr-tel (der)
decorous, be-kó-ved-ik
deep, tif

**defeat,** ma-pó-le (di)
**defect,** khe-sór-'n (der)
**definite,** ba-shtímt
**deft,** zí-kher
**(to) delete,** óys-shnayd-'n
**delicious,** ba-támt, ge-shmák, tam gan-éy-d'n
**(to) deliver,** tsú-shtel-en
**(to) demand,** fó-der-'n
**democracy,** de-mo-krá-ti-ye
**(to) denounce,** má-ser-'n
**dense,** ge-díkht
**dentist,** tsón-dok-ter (der)
**(to) deny,** léy-ken-en
**depends on,** ge-vént
**(to) deposit,** áyn-tsol-'n
**depraved,** far-dórb-'n
**depressed,** der-shlóg-'n
**(to) deride,** khóy-zek mákh-'n
**derision,** láy-tish ge-lékh-ter
**(to) describe,** ba-shráy-b'n
**desert,** míd-b'r (der)
**deserted,** pust, él-'nt
**(to) desire,** vél-en
**dessert,** tsí-mes (der)
**destined,** ba-shért
**destiny,** góy-r'l (der)
**destitute wretch,** oni v'-év-yon (der)
**destruction,** khúr-b'n (der)
**(to) detest,** faynt hób-'n
**developed,** ant-ví-kl't
**device,** makh-er-aý-ke (di)
**devil,** sót-'n (der), táy-v'l (der)
**devout,** frum
**diamond,** bril-yánt (der)
**diaspora,** gó-les (der)
**(to) die (animals),** péy-ger-'n
**(to) die,** shtárb-'n, tsú-makh-'n an oyg
**(to) die laughing,** hált-'n zikh bay di záyt-'n
**dietary regimen,** kásh-res (dos)
**different(ly),** án-dersh

**difficult**, shver
**(to) dig**, grób-'n
**(to) direct**, di-ri-gír-'n
**direct**, glaykh
**dirt**, shmuts (dos)
**(to) disappear**, far-shvínd-'n
**(to) disappear without a trace**, vi in vá-ser a-ráyn
**disappointed**, an-tóysht
**disaster**, ma-pó-le (di), úm-glik (der)
**(to) disclose**, óys-zog-'n
**(to) discover**, ant-dék-'n
**disease**, krenk (di)
**(to) disgust**, ékl-en
**disgusting**, mí-es, pas-kúd-ne, ék-'l-dik
**disgusting person**, pas-kud-nyák (der)
**dishes**, kéy-lim (di)
**(to) dislike**, faynt hób-'n
**dismayed**, an-tóysht
**(to) dismiss**, óp-loz-'n
**disorder**, hék-dish (der)
**(to) dispell**, tse-tráyb-'n
**(to) disperse**, tse-tráyb-'n
**(to) display**, váy-z'n
**(to) disrupt**, kál-ye mákh-'n
**(to) dissolve (legal)**, bót'l mákh-'n
**(to) distribute**, a-róys géb-'n, óys-teyl-'n
**(to) disturb**, shtér-en, tshép-'n
**(to) divide**, téyl-'n zikh, tse-téyl-'n
**divine spirit**, sh'-khí-ne (di)
**divorce**, get (der)
**divorced man**, góy-resh (der)
**divorcée**, g'rú-she (di)
**(to) do**, ton
**(to) do business**, hándl-en
**doctor**, dók-ter (der)
**dog**, hunt (der)
**doll**, bú-be-le, l'yál-ke (di)
**dolt**, shmi-gé-ge (der)
**domesticated animal**, be-héy-me (di)
**domestic bliss**, shó-l'm bá-yis

**(to) donate**, shénk-en
**donation**, ne-dó-ve (di)
**donkey**, éy-z'l (der)
**(to) do nothing**, a-rúm-gey- en léy-dik
**don't ask me!**, freg mikh bi-khéy-rem!
**(to) do without**, shpór-'n
**don't worry!**, nit ge-dáy-get
**door**, tir (di)
**doorpost scroll**, me-zú-ze (di)
**doubt**, só-fek (der)
**dough (baking)**, teyg (dos)
**dove**, toyb (di)
**down**, a-rún-ter
**dowry**, nád-'n (der)
**dozen**, tuts (der)
**(to) draw (attract)**, tsí-yen
**drawn out**, far-shlép-te krenk (di)
**dream**, khó-lem (der), troym (der)
**dress**, kleyd (dos)
**(to) dress**, ón-ton
**dressed**, ón-ge-ton
**dressed up**, óys-ge-putst
**dressing down**, mi she-béy-rekh
**dressmaker (fem.)**, shnáy-der-ke (di)
**(to) drink**, trink-'n
**drop**, tróp-'n (der)
**(to) drown**, der-trúnk-'n vér-'n
**drug**, me-di-tsín (di)
**drum**, poyk (di)
**drunkard**, shí-ker (der)
**dry**, trúk-'n
**duck**, kátsh-ke (di)
**dull**, on zalts un on fé-fer
**dummy**, góy-lem (der)
**dumpling (baked)**, k'nish (der)
**dumplings (boiled or fried)**, krép-lakh (di)
**dung**, drek (dos)
**dust**, shtoyb (der), mist (di)

# E

**each,** yé-der
**eager beaver,** tsú-tsig (der)
**ear,** óy-er (der)
**earlock,** péy-e (di)
**early,** fri
**early evening,** far-nákht
**(to) earn,** far-dín-en
**earring,** óy-er-ing-'l (der)
**earth,** erd (di)
**east,** míz-rakh
**easy,** gring
**easy mark,** shnuk (der)
**easy street,** shmálts-grib (der)
**(to) eat,** és-'n
**(to) eat like a glutton,** frés-'n
**(to) eavesdrop,** ún-ter-her-'n
**echo,** ví-der-kol (der)
**(to) educate,** der-tsíy-en
**education,** bíld-ung (di)
**egg,** béy-tse (di), ey (dos)
**eight,** akht
**eighteen,** ákht-s'n
**eighty,** ákht-sik
**either,** ó-der
**elbow,** él-en-bóy-g'n (der)
**(to) elect,** der-véyl-en
**elections,** vá-len (di)
**elementary school,** e-le-men-tár-shul (di)
**Elijah the Prophet,** ey-li-yó-u a-nó-vi
**elite,** p'ney (di), smé-te-ne (di)
**emaciated,** óys-ge-dart
**embarrassment,** bi-zó-y'n (der)
**(to) embezzle,** ba-gán-ven-en
**embittered,** far-bít-ert
**(to) embrace,** a-rúm-nem-en, háldz-'n
**emissary,** she-lí-akh (der)

**emotion,** ge-fíl (dos)
**employee (masc.),** ón-ge-shtelt-er (der), árb-i-ter (der)
**empty,** léy-dik, pust
**encounter,** ba-géy-gen-ish (dos)
**end,** sof (der)
**endless trouble,** hób-'n tsu zíng-'n un tsu zóg-'n
**enemy,** sóy-ne (der), faynt (der)
**engaged,** far-knást
**(to) engage in a sloppy or tedious job,** pátsh-k'n
**enlightenment movement,** has-kó-le (di)
**enough,** ge-núg
**(to) entertain,** a-mu-zír-'n
**(to) enthrone the bride,** ba-zéts-'n die ká-le
**entirely,** in gánts-'n
**envelope,** kon-vért (der)
**envy,** kín-e (di)
**(to) envy,** me-ká-ne zayn
**epoch,** tsayt (di)
**era,** tsay (di)
**(to) erase,** óys-mek-'n
**(to) erect,** óyf-boy-en, óyf-shtel-'n
**errand boy,** me-shó-res (der)
**especially,** dáv-ke, spe-tsi-él
**Eternal Light,** ner tó-mid (der)
**eternally,** éy-bik, tó-mid
**eternity,** éy-bi-kayt (di), óy-lem há-be (der)
**etiquette,** derkh-é-retz
**eulogy,** hés-ped (der)
**European Jews,** ash-ke-ná-zim (di)
**eve (of . . . ),** é-rev
**evening,** ó-v'nt (der)
**evening service,** má-riv
**event,** pa-sí-rung (di)
**even though,** a-fí-le
**every,** yé-der
**everyday,** vókh-e-dik
**everywhere,** u-me-túm, vu nor, i-ber-ál
**evil,** shlekht
**evil eye,** á-yin hó-re (der), sót-'n (der)
**evil inclination,** yéy-tser hó-re (der)

exactly, pínkt-lekh
exaggeration, í-ber-trayb-'n, bó-be máy-se (di)
example, mó-sh'l
(to) excavate, grób-'n
except for, a-khúts
excessive, í-ber-ig
(to) exchange, í-ber-bayt-'n
excitement, hu-há (der), tú-m'l (der)
excrement, drek (dos)
excuse, té-rets (der)
(to) excuse, móy-kh'l zayn, ant-shúl-dik-'n
exhausted, óys-ge-mutsh-et
(to) exist, fa-rán
(to) exorcise, óp-shprekh-'n
(to) expand, óys-tsi-yen
(to) expect, ríkh-t'n zikh
experienced, ge-pókt un ge-mózl-'t
expert, méy-vin (der)
(to) expire, óys-gey-en
(to) explain, óys-tay-nen zikh
explanation, taytsh (der), sí-be (di)
(to) explode, pláts-'n
explosion, shos (der), óyf-rays (der)
(to) extend, óys-tsiy-en, tsíy-en
eye, oyg (der)
eyebrows, brém-en (di)
eyeglasses, bríl-'n (di)
eyelashes, ví-yes (di)

# F

**fabrication,** lig-'n (der)
**face,** pó-nim (dos)
**factory,** fa-brík (di)
**(to) fade,** far-géy-'n
**(to) fail,** ún-ter-geyn
**failed,** me-khú-le
**failing, (shortcoming),** khe-só-r'n
**(to) fail to . . . ,** far-féyl-en
**failure,** dúrkh-fal (der)
**(to) faint,** khá-lesh-'n
**faint hearted one,** lé-mish-ke (di)
**faith,** bi-tókh-'n (der), glóyb-'n (dos), tsú-troy (der)
**faithful,** ge-tráy
**faker,** fón-fer (der)
**(to) fall,** fál-en
**fallen one,** ge-fál-e-ner (der)
**false piety,** got di ne-shó-me shúld-ik
**family,** mish-pó-khe (di)
**family member,** kó-rev (der)
**famous,** ón-ge-zey-en, ba-vúst
**far,** vayt
**farmer,** póy-er (der)
**(to) fast,** fást-'n
**fast day,** tó-nes (der)
**fat,** fet, grob
**fat (animal),** shmalts (der)
**fat chance,** folg mir a gang
**fate,** góy-r'l (der), máz-l (dos)
**fated,** ba-shért
**father,** fót-'r, tá-te (der)
**father dear,** tá-te-nyu
**father-in-law,** shver (der)
**fault,** khe-só-r'n (der)
**favor,** tóy-ve (di)
**fear,** móy-re (di), shrek (der)
**Feast of Lights,** khá-ni-ke

110

**Feast of Tabernacles,** sú-kes
**Feast of Weeks,** she-ví- es
**feather bed,** pé-re-ne (di)
**February,** féb-ru-ar
**(to) feel (touch),** a tap ton
**feeling,** ge-fíl (dos), khush (der)
**fell in over his head,** a-ráyn-ge-fal-'n vi a yov-'n in sú-ke; íber-'n kop
**fellow,** bókh-er (der)
**fellows,** khév-re (di), bo-khí-rim (di)
**female,** ne-kéy-ve (di)
**Festival of Rejoicing in the Law,** sím-khes tóy-re
**festive,** yón-tev-dig, fréy-lakh
**festive meal,** sú- de (di)
**fever,** hits (di)
**fifteen,** fúf-ts'n
**fifty,** fúf-tsik
**(to) figure,** rékh-nen
**filled fish,** ge-fíl-te fish
**final,** énd-gilt-ig, tsu-létst
**(to) find,** ge-fín-en
**fine,** sheyn, din (as in fine sugar)
**fine Jew,** shéyn-er yid (der)
**finger,** fín-ger (der)
**finished,** oys, ge-énd-ikt
**fire,** fáy-er (der)
**fire!,** es brent
**firearms,** ge-vér (dos)
**firm (business),** fír-me (di)
**fish,** fish (der)
**fishwife,** kho-lé-ri-ye (di), (lit., cholera)
**fitting,** pás-ik
**five,** finf
**Five Books of Moses,** khú-mesh (der), tóy-re (di)
**flatiron,** prés-'l (dos)
**(to) flatter,** shméy-kh'l-en
**flattery,** kha-ní-fe
**flesh,** fleysh (dos)
**flirt,** tsáts-ke (di)
**flood,** máb-'l (der)
**floor,** dil (der), pad-ló-ge (di)

**flop (play, book, etc.)**, shmá-te (di)
**flour**, mel (di)
**fluffy**, púkh-ke
**flute**, fleyt (di)
**fly**, flig (di)
**(to) fly**, flíy-en
**fog**, né-p'l (der)
**fold**, kneytsh (der)
**folk**, folk (dos)
**(to) follow after**, nókh-gey-en
**food**, és-'n (dos)
**food treat**, máy-khl (dos)
**fool**, be-héy-me (di), nar (der), shle-míl (der), shme-gé-ge (der), yold (der), shtik be-héy-me (di)
**foolish**, nár-ish
**foot**, fus (der)
**for**, tsu-líb
**for all it's worth**, oyf vus di velt shteyt
**forbidden by Jewish dietary law**, treyf
**forehead**, shtern (der)
**forest**, vald (der)
**forever**, éy-bik
**for example**, li-mó-sh'l, tsum báy-shpil
**forfend**, kho-lí-le
**(to) forget**, far-gés-'n
**forget it**, móy-kh'l
**(to) forgive**, móy-kh'l zayn
**fork**, góp-'l (der)
**forlorn**, pust un pas
**fornication**, hu-re-ráy (di)
**fortunate**, máz-'l-dig
**fortune**, far-méy-g'n
**forty**, fér-tsik
**(to) foul things up**, far-báyt-'n di yóyts-res
**(to) founder**, ún-ter-gey-en
**four**, fir
**Four Questions**, fir ká-shes
**fourteen**, fér-ts'n
**fragrance**, réy-akh (der), ge-rúkh (der)
**fraud**, shvínd-'l (der)

**fraudulent**, g'-néy-vish
**free**, héf-ker, fray
**free of charge**, um-zíst
**(to) freeze**, frír-'n
**fresh**, frish, (not for impertinent)
**Friday**, fráy-tik
**friend (masc.)**, fraynt (der), kháv-'r (der)
**friend (fem.)**, fraynd-í-ne (di), khá-v'r-te (di)
**friendly**, fráynt-lakh
**friendship**, fráynt-shaft (di)
**fright**, shrek (der)
**(to) frighten**, í-ber-shrek-'n
**from**, fun
**frost**, kelt (di)
**fruit dessert**, kom-pót (der)
**fruit stew**, tsí-mes (der)
**full**, ful
**full detail**, mit á-le pítch-ev-kes
**full-grown**, ful-kóm
**fully developed**, ful-kóm
**funeral**, li-vá-ye (di)
**fur**, pelts (der)
**fur hat**, spodik (der)
**furniture**, mé-b'l (di)
**fury**, tsorn (der)
**fuss**, hu-há (der)
**future**, mór-g'n (der), tsú-kunft (der)

# G

**gall**, gal (di), khúts-pe (di) (id.)
**gallbladder**, gal (di)
**gallows**, t'lí-ye (di)
**galoshes**, ka-lósh-'n (di)
**game**, shpil (di)
**gang**, khév-re
**gangster**, khév-re-man (der)
**garb**, kléyd-ung (di)
**garbage**, shmuts (der)
**garden**, górt-'n (der)
**Garden of Eden**, gan éyd-'n
**garlic**, knób-'l (der)
**garret**, bóy-dem (der)
**gas**, gaz (di)
**gasoline**, naft (der)
**(to) gather**, zám-len
**gathering**, far-zám-lung (di)
**generation**, dor (der)
**gentile (masc.)**, shéy-gets (der), goy (der)
**gentile (fem.)**, shík-se (di), góy-e (di)
**gentle**, éy-d'l, tsart
**(to) get it over with**, óp-kum-en
**get on with it**, a-klál
**(to) get up in a foul mood**, óyf-shtey-en oyf der línk-er zayt
**giant**, riz (der)
**gift**, ma-tó-ne (di)
**gift of gab**, pisk (der)
**(to) give**, géb-'n
**(to) give away**, shénk'n
**(to) give back**, óp-geb'n
**gizzard**, pú-pik (der)
**glance**, blik (der)
**glass**, gloz (di)
**gloom**, khmár-e (di), ú-met-i-kayt (di)
**gloomy**, ú-me-tik, tróy-er-ik
**glutton**, frés-er (der), khá-z'r (der)

114

**(to) go,** géy-en
**(to) go all out,** lég'n zikh in der leng un der breyt
**(to) go away,** a-vék géy-en
**go bang your head on the wall,** gey shray khay ve-ká-yom
**God,** got, a-do-nóy, a-do-shém, ha-shém
**God bless you,** tsu ge-zúnt
**godfather (at circumcision),** sán-dik (der)
**God forbid,** got zol óp-hit-'n; khas ve-kho-lí-le
**God willing,** im yír-tse ha-shém
**gold,** gold (dos)
**golden land (America),** góld-i-ne me-dí-ne (di)
**gone,** a-vék
**good,** gut
**good buy,** bí-lik vi borsht, me-tsí-ye (di)
**good-bye,** a gút-'n tog
**good deed,** míts-ve (di)
**good evening,** gút'n óv-n't
**good for him,** a míts-ve oyf im
**good for nothing,** tóy-g'n oyf ka-pó-res
**good for you,** a léyb-'n in dir
**good luck,** máz'l (dos)
**good luck,** maz-'l tov
**good morning,** gut mór-g'n
**good night,** gút-e nakht
**good wish for success,** mít-'n rékht-'n fis
**goose,** ganz (di)
**gossip,** losh'n hó-re (dos), re-khí-les (dos)
**gossip (person),** yén-te (di)
**go to hell,** gey in d'rerd, in d'rerd a-ráyn, tsu ál-de shvárts-e ríkh-es
**government,** re-gí-rung (di)
**(to) grab,** óys-khap-'n
**granchild,** éy-nik-'l (dos)
**grandfather,** zéy-de (der)
**grandmother,** bó-be (di)
**grape,** váyn-troyb (di)
**grass,** groz (dos)
**great distance,** me-há-lakh (der)
**greedy one,** khá-z'r (der)
**green,** grin
**(to) greet,** ba-grís-'n

grief, tróy-er (der)
(to) grieve, tróy-er-'n
(to) gripe, grízh-'n
groom, khó-s'n (der)
ground, erd (di)
group, khév-re (di)
(to) grow up, óys-vaks-'n, ún-ter-vaks-'n
grudge, síne (di)
(to) grumble, búr-tsh'n, grí-zh'n
(to) guard, hít-'n, óp-hit-'n
(to) guess, tréf-'n
guest, gast (der), óy-rekh (der)
gullet, gór-g'l (der)
gypsy, tsi-gáy-ner (der)

# H

**habit,** ge-vóyn-hayt (di)
**hag,** klí-pe (di)  ma-khe-shéy-fe (di)
**haggler,** yákh-ne (di)
**hair,** hor (der)
**half,** halb, helft
**half-wit,** shtik be-héy-me, yold (der)
**hamburger,** kot-lét (der)
**hamlet,** dorf (der), yí-shuv (der)
**hammer,** há-mer (der)
**hand,** hant (di)
**handkerchief,** nóz-tikh-'l (dos)
**handsome,** sheyn
**Hanukkah,** khá-ni-ke
**hapless one,** shme-gé-ge (der)
**(to) happen,** ge-shéyn
**happiness,** glik (dos), freyd (dos)
**happy,** fréy-lakh, glík-lakh
**happy event,** sím-khe (di)
**Happy New Year,** l'shó-ne tóy-ve, a gut yor
**hardly,** mish-téyns gezogt
**harridan,** kho-lé-ri-ye (di)
**hasidic leader,** ré-be (der)
**(to) hate,** faynt hób-'n
**hatred,** sí-ne (di), has (der)
**haughty,** shtayf
**(to) have,** hob'n
**(to) have a say,** hób-'n a déy-e
**(to) have become lost,** far-fál-'n ge-vór-'n, far-blón-zhet
**(to) have enough,** klék-'n
**have it your way,** zol zayn a-zóy
**(to) have misplaced something,** far-fál-'n ge-vór-'n
**he,** er
**head,** kop (der)
**(to) heal,** héyl-'n, óys-heyl-'n
**health,** ge-zúnt (dos)
**(to) hear,** hér-'n

(to) hear out, óys-her-'n
heart, harts (dos)
heart of the matter, der-í-ker
Heaven forbid, khás ve-shó-l'm, kho-lí-le
heavens, hím-l (der)
heavy, shver
Hebrew, he-bréy-ish
Hebrew School, tál-mid tóy-re (di)
hedonist, a-pi-kóy-res (der)
heel, p'-yá-te (di)
heir, yóy-resh (der)
hell, ge-hé-nem (der)
hello, shó-l'm a léy-khem
hell on wheels, gey-'n oyf ré-der-'n
help, ge-váld
help, hilf (di)
(to) help, hélf-'n
her (to her, or her's), ir
here, a-hér, do
hero, held (der)
heroism, ge-vú-re (di)
hidden, ba-hált-'n
(to) hide, ba-hált-'n
high pressure salesmanship, aýn-red-n a kind in boykh
high school, mít-'l-shul (di)
highwayman, gáz-l'n (der)
hill, barg (der)
(to) him, im
(to) hinder, kál-ye mákh-'n
history, ge-shíkh-te (di)
(to) hit, shlóg-'n
hoarse, héyz-rig
hodgepodge, mísh-mash (der)
(to) hold, a-rúm-ne-men, hált-'n
hole, lokh (der)
hole in the head, lokh in kop
holiday, yón-tev (der)
holiday eve, é-rev yón-tev
holiday prayer book, mákh-z'r (der)
holocaust, khúr-b'n (der)

**holy,** héy-lik
**holy ark,** ó-r'n kóy-desh
**Holy Scriptures, (Jewish),** ta-nákh
**Holy Temple (in Jerusalem),** beys-a-mík-desh (der)
**home (going, or homeward),** a-héym
**home,** dí-re (di), shtub (di), hoyz (di)
**homemaker (skilled),** brí-ye (di)
**(to be) homesick,** bénk-'n
**homey,** héym-ish
**homiletical anthology,** méd-resh (der)
**homosexual,** féy-ge-le (dos)
**honest,** ér-lekh
**honey,** hón-ik (der)
**honeyed dough confectionary,** téyg-lakh (di)
**honor,** kí-bed (der)
**(to) honor,** me-khá-bed zayn
**honorable,** ér-lekh, láy-tish
**honored,** ón-ge-zey-en
**honor of beginning reading of Torah Scroll,** khó-s'n b'réy-shis (der)
**honor of concluding reading of Torah Scroll,** khó-s'n tóy-re (der)
**hoosegow,** khad-gád-ye (der), túr-me (di)
**(to) hope,** hóf-'n
**hopefully,** ha-le-váy
**horse,** ferd (der)
**horseradish,** kh'-réyn (der)
**horseshoe,** pít-ko-ve (di)
**hospital,** shpi-túl (der)
**hospitality,** kí-bed (der), gást-fraynd-lich-kayt (dos)
**hot,** heys
**hour,** sho (di)
**house,** hoyz (di), shtub (di)
**householder,** bal-e-bós (der)
**housekeeper (skilled),** bér-i-ye (di)
**house of study,** bes-méd-resh (der)
**house slippers,** shték-shikh
**how,** vi a-zóy
**how are you,** vi halt es mit aykh
**how come,** vi kumt es, staytsh
**how far,** vi vayt
**how long,** vi lang

**how many**, vi-fíl
**how much**, vi-fíl
**however**, ó-ber
**huckleberry**, tshér-ni-tse (di)
**human being**, né-fish (der), mentsh (der)
**(to) humiliate**, far-shém-en
**humility**, a-ní-ves (dos)
**hundred**, hún-dert
**hunger**, hún-ger (der)
**hunger constantly**, ún-ter-hung-er'n
**hungry**, hún-ge-rik

# I

**I**, ikh
**I couldn't care less,** mayn bó-bes dáy-ge, es geyt mir nit on
**idea,** áyn-fal (der)
**idle,** pust un pas
**idler,** léy-di-gey-er (der)
**if,** az, oyb
**illegible scrawl,** kó-tshi-res mit ló-pe-tes
**illiterate,** am-ó-rets (der)
**illness,** krenk (di)
**(to) imitate,** nókh-makh-'n
**immediately,** téy-kef
**immigrant,** grín-er (der)
**impertinent,** khúts-pe-dik
**important,** víkh-tik, ón-ge-zen
**impossible,** um-még-likh
**impudent arrogance,** khúts-pe (di)
**in (to),** a-ráyn
**in a bad way,** oyf ge-hók-te tsó-res
**income,** par-nó-se (di), hakh-nó-se (di)
**inebriated,** shí-ker
**ineffective,** (id.) hélf-'n vi a tóy-t'n bán-kes
**inept one,** kál-yi-ke (der)
**inept person,** shle-míl (der)
**inexpensive,** bí-lik
**infant,** éy-fe-le (dos)
**influential one,** mákh-er (der)
**inheritance,** ye-rú-she (di)
**in honor of,** li-kó-ved
**ink,** tint (di)
**in-law (fem.),** me-khe-té-nes-te (di)
**in-law (masc.),** me-khít-'n (der)
**innocent,** úm-shul-dig
**in order that . . . ,** k'dey
**in peace,** b'shó-lem
**insane,** me-shú-ge, tsu-dréyt
**inside,** ín-e-vey-nig

**instant,** ré-ge (di)
**(to) instruct,** ón-zog-'n
**insufficient,** karg
**(to) insult,** ba-léy-dik-'n
**intelligent,** klug
**intermediate days of festivals,** kho-le-móyd
**(to) interrupt,** í-ber-rays-'n
**intestine,** kísh-ke (di)
**in that case,** me-khe-téy-se
**in vain,** um-zíst
**(to) invent,** óys-kleı ı
**inventory,** khésh-b'n (der), rékh-nung (der)
**(to) investigate,** fórsh-'n
**(to) invite,** far-bét-'n, áyn-lad-'n
**IOU,** vék-s'l (der)
**is,** iz
**Israelite,** yis-ról
**(to) itch,** báys-'n, kráts-'n
**it doesn't matter,** es makht nit oys
**it is beneath me,** es shteyt mir nit on
**it won't hurt him to . . . ,** nit krank tsu . . .

# J

**jail**, t'fí-se (di), túr-me (di)
**January**, yá-nu-ar
**jealousy**, éy-fer-zukht (di), kín-e (di)
**Jerusalem**, ye-ru-sho-lá-yim
**Jew (masc.)**, yid (der)
**jewel**, bril-yánt (der)
**jewelry**, tsí-rung (di)
**Jewess**, yíd-e-ne
**Jewish court**, béz-din (der)
**Jewishness**, yíd-ish-kayt (dos)
**Jewish religious knowledge**, tóy-re
**Jew of German descent**, yé-ke (der)
**Jews from Central and Eastern Europe**, ash-ke-ná-zim (di)
**jibe**, shtokh (der)
**job**, shtél-e (di), ár-bet (di)
**joke**, shpas (der), vits (der)
**journalist**, zhur-na-líst (der)
**joy**, freyd (di)
**Judaism**, yíd-ish-kayt (dos)
**(to) judge**, pás-ke-nen
**judge**, ríkht-er (der)
**judgment**, ge-ríkht (dos), p'sak (der), mish-pet (der)
**juice**, zaft (der)
**July**, yú-li
**(to) jump**, shpríng-en
**June**, yú-ni
**junk**, kha-zer-áy (dos)
**junk food**, no-sher-áy (dos)
**just because . . .** , glat a-zóy
**justice**, ge-rékht-i-kayt (di), yóy-sher (der)

# K

**(to) keep,** hált-'n
**(to) keep silent,** hált-'n dos moyl
**kerosene,** naft (der)
**key,** shlís-'l (der)
**kidneys,** ní-r'n (di)
**(to) kill,** der-hár-gen-en
**kind,** sort (der)
**kindergarten,** kind-er-górt-'n (der)
**(to) kindle,** ón-tsind-'n
**kindness,** tóy-ve (di)
**king,** méy-lakh (der)
**kiss,** kush (der)
**kitchen,** kikh (di)
**knee,** kni (der)
**knife,** més-er (der)
**knot,** knip (der)
**(to) know,** kén-en
**knowledge,** ví-s'n-shaft (di)
**Kohen,** koyn (der)
**kosher,** kó-sh'r

# L

labor, ár-bet (di)
laborer, ár-bet-'r (der)
lad, ying'l (dos)
lady, dá-me (di)
lake, taykh (der)
lame, krum
landowner (East. Europe), pó-rets (der)
large, groys
lascivious, óys-ge-las'n
(to) last, ge-dóyr-'n
late, shpet, far-zá-men
(to) laugh, lákh-'n
laughter through tears, lákh-'n mit yásh-tshe-kes
(to) launder, óys-vash-'n
laundry, vesh (dos)
law, din (der), ge-bót (dos), ge-zéts (dos)
law abiding, áyn-shten-dik
law and commentary compendium, tal-mud (der)
law, tradition of, ha-ló-khe
lawyer, ad-vo-kát (der)
lazy, foyl
lead (mineral), blay
(to) lead, fír-'n
(to) lead by the nose, fír-'n far der noz
leaf, blat (der)
(to) leak, rín-en
lean, mó-ger
(to) learn, óys-lern-en
learned one, tál-mid khó-khem
leaven, khó-mets (der)
lecture, lék-tsi-ye (di)
(to the) left, links
leg, fus (der)
leg (furniture), fís'l (dos)
legacy, ye-rú-she (di)
legal, kósh-'r
less, véy-nik-er

**lesson,** lék-tsi-ye (di)
**let it pass,** zol mayns í-ber-geyn
**let's get on with it,** a-klál
**letter (of the alphabet),** oys (der)
**letter (mail),** briv (der)
**lettuce,** sa-lát (der)
**let us,** ló-mir
**Levite,** léy-vi (der)
**lewd,** óys-ge-las'n
**(to) liberate,** ba-fráy-en
**lie,** líg-n (der)
**(to) lie (as on a bed),** líg-'n
**life,** léb-'n (dos)
**life in this world,** óy-lem há-ze
**(to) lift up,** óyf-heyb-'n
**lightning,** blits (der)
**(to) like,** gláykh-'n
**limit,** shir (der)
**(to) limp,** hínk-en
**linen,** láy-v'nt (dos)
**liquor,** brón-f'n (der)
**listen!,** hert
**listlessly,** on khéy-shek
**lithe,** shlank
**little,** bí-s'l
**little by little,** bís-lekh-vays
**liturgical petition for God's help,** mi-she-béy-rakh
**livelihood,** par-nó-se (di)
**lively,** lé-be-dik
**liver (anat.),** lé-ber (di)
**loaf (small),** búl-ke (di)
**loafer,** léy-dik-gey-er (der)
**lock,** shlos (der)
**(to) look,** kúk-'n
**(to) look for,** zúkh-'n
**(to) look like,** óys-zey-en
**look out,** hit zikh
**(to) look over,** í-ber-kuk-'n
**(to) lose one's way,** far-blón-zhen
**lost opportunity,** far-fál-'n

**lotion,** shmír-akhts (dos)
**loudmouth,** pisk (der)
**loudmouth,** yákh-ne (di)
**love,** líb-e (di)
**(to) love,** lib hób-'n
**lover,** ka-va-lyér (der), lib hób-'r (der)
**low,** ge-méyn, níd-rik
**low character,** dóv-'r ákh-'r (der), prost
**lower back area,** krí-zhés (di)
**loyal,** ge-tráy
**luck,** glik (dos)
**lucky,** glík-lakh, máz-'l-dik
**lumber,** holts (dos)
**lung,** lung (di)
**luscious,** záft-ik

# M

machine, ma-shín (di)
mad, me-shú-ge, beyz
madman, me-shú-ge-ner (der)
madness, me-shú-gas (dos)
magic, kí-shef (der)
maiden, méy-d'l (dos), b'sú-le (di)
maid servant, dinst (di)
mail, post (di)
(to) make, mákh-'n
(to) make a bed, óys-bet-'n
(to) make a commotion, mákh-'n a túm-'l
(to) make a fuss over, mákh-'n a tsí-mes
(to) make an empty threat, strá-sh-'n di genz
(to) make a payment, áyn-tsol-'n
(to) make fun of, khóy-zik mákh-'n
(to) make null and void, bót-'l mákh-'n
(to) make Sabbath preparations, mákh-'n shá-bes
(to) make the acquaintance of, ba-kén-en zikh
(to) make up, í-ber-bet-'n
malcontent, kvetsh (der)
man, man (der)
man about town, ka-val-yér (der)
manipulator, mákh-er (der)
manner, óyf-'n (der)
man servant, me-shó-res (der)
(to) manufacture, mákh-'n, óys-ar-bet-'n
many, a sakh
mantle for Torah, mén-t'l (dos)
marauder, gáz-l'n (der)
March, marts
marked, mark (der)
marriage canopy, khú-pe (di)
marriage contract, k'sú-be (di)
(to) marry, khá-se-ne hób-'n
(to) marry off, khá-se-ne mákh-'n
martyrdom, kí-dish-a-shem
Master of the Universe, ri-bóy-ne shel óyl-'m

128

matchmaker, shád-kh'n (der)
mathematics, ma-te-má-tik (di)
matso ball, knéy-d'l (di)
matso omelet, mát-se bray
May (month), may
maybe, éf-sher
may his name be blotted out, yi-mákh sh-móy
may you live a long life, biz hún-dert un tsván-tsik
(to) me, mir
meantime, der-váy-le
meat, fleysh (dos)
meat food (in dietary laws), fléysh-ik
meat market, fléysh-mark (der)
meat which satisfies the strictest ritual inspection, glat kó-sh'r
(to) meddle, a-ráyn mísh-'n zikh
meddler, kí-bi-tser (der)
medicine, me-di-tsín (di)
meeting (as one meets another), ba-géy-gen-ish (dos)
meeting (organizational), zíts-ung (di)
melody, ní-g'n (der)
melon, me-lón (der)
member, mít-glid (der)
memento, án-denk (der)
memorial prayer, eyl mó-ley
memorial service, yíz-k'r
memory, zi-kó-r'n (der)
mentally unbalanced, ge-rírt
merchant, sóy-kher (der)
mercy, rakh-mó-nes
merit, máy-le (di), z'-khús (der)
message, b'sú-re (di)
messenger, shík-ying-'l (der)
Messiah, me-shí-akh (der)
Messianic era, me-shí-akhs tsáyt-'n
midwife, várts-froy (di)
milk, milkh (di)
million, mil-yón (der)
miracle, nes (der)
mire, bló-te (di)
miser, kám-ts'n (der), kárg-er (der)
misfit, shle-míl (der)

**misfortune,** shlak (der), úm-glik (der)
**(to) mislead,** far-fír-'n
**missing,** ni-tó
**mister,** reb
**(to) mix up,** tsu-mísh-'n
**mode of dress,** me-há-lakh (der)
**(to) molest,** tshép-'n
**moment,** ré-ge (di), mo-mént (der)
**Monday,** món-tik
**money,** gelt (dos), mat-béy-e (di), me-zú-men (dos)
**money cache,** kníp'l (dos)
**monkey,** mál-pe (di)
**month,** mó-nat (der)
**moon,** le-vó-ne (di)
**more,** mer
**more power to you,** yásh-'r kóy-akh
**morning,** in-der-frí (der), mór-g'n (der), fri (der)
**mother,** mú-ter (di)
**mother-in-law,** shví-g'r
**mother tongue,** má-me lósh-'n
**mountain,** barg (der)
**(to) mourn,** klóg-'n, tróy-er-'n
**mourner,** ó-v'l (der)
**mourners' doxology,** ká-dish (der)
**mourning,** tróy-er (der)
**mourning period of 7 days,** shí-ve
**mourning period of 30 days,** shlóy-shim
**mouse,** moyz (di)
**moustache,** vón-tse (di)
**mouth,** moyl (dos), pisk (der)
**(to) move,** rír-'n
**movement,** ba-véy-gung (di)
**moving (emotionally),** rír-'n-dik
**mud,** bló-te (di)
**(to) murder,** der-hárg-en-en
**mushrooms,** shvém-lakh (di)
**music,** mu-zík (di)
**musician (instrumentalist),** kléz-mer (der), mú-zi-ker (der)
**music notation,** nót-'n (di)
**mute,** shtum

# N

**nag,** klí-pe (di)
**(to) nag,** díl-'n a kop
**nail,** nóg-'l (der)
**nail (in construction),** tsvuk (der)
**name,** nó-men (der)
**(to be) named,** héys-'n
**nap,** drém'l (der)
**narrow,** shmol
**nation,** folk (dos)
**navel,** pú-pik (der)
**near,** léf-'n
**nearby,** nó-ent
**(to) need,** dárf-'n
**needle,** nód-'l (di)
**(to) needle,** grízh-'n
**ne'er-do-well,** óys-vorf (der)
**neighbor (fem.),** sh'-khéy-ne (di)
**neighbor (masc.),** shó-kh-'n (der)
**nephew,** pli-mé-nik (der)
**net price,** ún-tersh-te shú-re (di)
**neutral food (in dietary laws),** pá-re-ve
**nevertheless,** b'méy-le
**new month,** rosh khóy-desh
**news,** ná-yes (di)
**newspaper,** tsáyt-ung (di)
**New Year,** ro-she-shó-ne
**next door,** tir tsu tir
**niece,** pli-mé-ni-tse (di)
**nine,** nayn
**nineteen,** náyn-ts'n
**ninety,** náyn-tsik
**Ninth of Ab,** tísh-e bov
**no,** neyn
**noble,** éy-d'l
**nobleman,** pó-rets (der)
**noblewoman,** prí-tse (di)

**(the) nobody**, shmén-drik (der), shnuk (der)
**noise**, tú-m'l (der), ta-ra-ràm (der)
**noisemaker**, grág-er (der)
**nonbeliever**, a-pi-kóy-res (der)
**none**, kayn
**nonsense**, shtus (der)
**noodles flakes**, fár-f'l (di)
**noodles**, lók-sh'n (di)
**no one**, kéy-ner
**north**, tsóf-'n
**nose**, noz (di)
**nosy person**, yén-te (di)
**not any**, kayn
**not at all**, neḱht-ik-er tog
**not bad**, nish-ḱo-she
**not enough**, vey-nik
**nothing**, gór-nit
**(to) notice**, ba-mérk-'n
**(to) notify**, rúf-'n
**novel**, ro-mán (der)
**November**, no-vém-ber
**now**, itst
**nowhere**, in-ér-gets nit
**nuisance**, ón-shik-e-nesh (dos)
**number**, nú-mer (der)
**nutcracker**, knák-nis-'l

# O

oaf, bul-ván (der)
oath, shvú-e (di)
occasion, ge-lé-g'n-hayt (di)
occupied, far-nú-men
ocean, yam (der)
o'clock, a-zéy-ger
October, ok-tó-ber
oculist, óyg-'n-dok-ter (der)
odd, mód-ne
odor, réy-akh (der)
often, oft
oil (edible), bóy-m'l
oil (nonedible), naft (der)
ointment, shmír-akhts (dos)
old, alt
old folks home, móy-shev z'kéy-nim (der)
old maid, ál-te moyd (di)
old man, zók-'n (der)
old wives' tale, bó-be máy-se (di)
omelet, fáyn-kukh-'n (der)
omen, sí-men (der)
on, oyf
once, a-mól
once upon a time, a-mól
one, eyns
one of the boys, khév-re-man (der)
one's self, zikh
onion, tsí-be-le (di)
onlooker, kí-bi-tser (der)
only one, éyn-tsik-er (der)
on pins and needles, oyf shpíl-kes
on tiptoe, oyf di shpits fíng-er
open, óf-'n
(to) open up, óyf-makh-'n
opinion, méy-nung (der)
opponent, mis-ná-ged (der)

**opportunity**, ge-lé-gen-hayt (di)
**(to) oppress**, un-ter-drík-'n
**option**, bréy-re (di)
**optometrist**, óp-ti-ker (der)
**or**, ó-der
**orange (fruit)**, ma-ránts (der)
**orator**, dársh-'n (der), réd-ner (der)
**order**, ba-fél (der)
**(to) order**, ba-shtél-'n
**ordinarily**, ge-véynt-likh
**organ (anat.)**, glid (dos)
**organ (musical)**, ór-gil (der)
**orgasm**, or-gás-'m (der)
**oriental Jews**, se-fár-dim
**orphanage**, beys ye-sóy-mim (der)
**others**, án-de-re (di)
**out**, oys
**outcry**, ge-shréy (dos)
**outhouse**, óp-tret (der)
**outlandish**, me-shú-ge
**out of**, a-róys
**out of one's mind**, a-róp fun zín-en
**out of work**, a-rúm-géy-en léy-dig
**outside of**, a-khúts
**outsider**, frémd-er (der)
**oven**, óy-v'n (der)
**over**, a-rí-ber
**overbearing person**, á-zes pó-nim (der)
**overcoat**, man-t'l (der) óy-ber-man-t'l (der)
**(to) overhear**, ún-ter-her-'n
**overshoes**, ka-lósh-n (di)
**overweight**, záft-ig
**(to) own**, far-móg-n
**owner**, bal-e-bós (der), ey-g'n-ti-mer (der)

# P

**pack**, pék-'l (dos)
**(to) pack**, pák-'n
**page**, blat (der)
**pain**, véy-tik (der)
**pair**, pór-'l (dos)
**pale**, bleykh
**palm branch**, lú-lev (der)
**pancake**, lát-ke (di)
**paper**, pa-pír (dos)
**paradise**, gan éyd'n
**parcel**, pék-'l (dos)
**part**, teyl (der)
**(to) participate**, án-teyl né-men
**Passover**, péy-sakh
**Passover festive meal**, séy-der (der)
**(to) pass the time**, far-bréng-'n di tsayt
**past**, far-gáng-en-hayt (di)
**pastry**, ge-béks (dos)
**patch**, lá-te (di)
**patience**, ge-dúld (di)
**pauper**, káb-ts'n (der), o-re-mán (der)
**(to) paw**, a tap ton, tap-'n
**(to) pay**, ba-tsól-'n, tsól-'n
**(to) pay a condolence call**, me-ná-khem ó-v'l zayn
**(to) pay out (in installments)**, óys-tsol-'n
**pea**, bé-b'l (dos), ár-bes (der)
**peace**, fríd-'n (der), shó-l'm (der)
**peaceful**, rú-ik
**peach**, feŕsh-ke (di)
**pear**, bar (di)
**pelt**, pelts (der)
**penis**, pots, (der), shmok (der)
**penitent**, bal t'shú-ve (der)
**Pentateuch**, khú-mesh (der)
**people**, folk (dos)
**pepper**, fé-fer (der)

**performance,** fór-shtel-ung (di), shpil (di)
**perhaps,** éf-sher, mes-tá-me
**(to) perish,** úm-kum-en
**permitted,** tór-en, még-'n
**permitted (clean) food,** kó-sh'r
**person,** mensh
**Pesah,** péy-sakh
**(to) pester,** díl-'n a kop, der-géy-en di yór-'n, tshép-'n
**(to) pet,** glét-'n
**petroleum,** naft (der)
**pharmacist,** ap-téy-ker (der)
**phew,** fe
**philosophy,** fi-li-só-fi-ye (di)
**phobia,** me-shu-gás (dos)
**phylacteries,** t'fí-lin (di)
**(to) pick,** kláyb-'n
**pickle,** zóy-e-re ú-ger-ke (di)
**picture,** bild (dos)
**piece,** shtik (der)
**pin,** shpíl-ke (di)
**pinch,** knip (der)
**pink,** ró-ze
**pioneer,** khó-luts (der), pi-yo-nír (der)
**pious,** frum
**pious one,** khó-sid (der)
**pity,** rakh-mó-nes
**place,** ort (dos), plats (der)
**plague,** ma-géy-fe (di), má-ke (di)
**plain,** prost
**plain talk,** má-me lósh-'n
**(to) plant (false evidence),** ún-ter-varf-'n
**plate,** té-ler (der)
**platform,** bí-ne (di)
**(to) play,** shpíl-'n
**(to) play a dirty trick,** óp-ton oyf térk-ish
**playing cards,** kórt-'n (di)
**plaything,** tsáts-ke (di)
**please,** zayt a-zóy gut
**(to) please,** ge-fél-'n
**pleasure,** ná-khes (dos)

**pleasure,** me-khá-ye
**pliers,** ts'-váng (di)
**plum,** floym (di)
**(to) plunder,** ba-rá-be-v'n
**pocket,** ké-she-ne (di)
**poem,** lid (dos)
**point,** shpits (der)
**pointer,** váy-zer (der)
**(to) poison,** far-sám-en
**poke,** shtoys (der)
**police,** po-li-tséy (di)
**poor,** ó-rem
**poor craftsman,** kál-yi-ke (der)
**poorhouse,** hék-dish (der)
**poor man,** o-re-mán (der)
**(of) poor quality,** drek (dos)
**poor slob,** shlép-er (der), shli-má-z'l (der)
**poor tasting,** es hot mayn bó-bes tam
**poor thing,** né-fish (der)
**porch,** gá-nik (der)
**porridge,** lé-mish-ke (di)
**portent,** sí-men (der)
**position,** shtél-e (di)
**positively,** a-vá-de
**possibly,** éf-sher
**(to) postpone,** óp-leyg-'n
**pot,** tep-'l (dos), top (der)
**potato,** búl-be (di), kar-tó-f'l (di)
**pot roast,** ró-s'l-fleysh (der)
**poverty,** dá-lis (der), ó-rem-kayt (di)
**practical matters,** tákh-lis
**(to) pray,** dá-ven-en
**prayer,** t'fí-le (di)
**prayer book,** sí-der (der)
**prayer leader,** bal t'fí-le  (der)
**prayer shawl,** tá-lis (der)
**(to) pray successfully,** óys-bet-'n
**preacher,** dársh-'n (der)
**predestined marriage partner,** zí-vig (der)
**(to) prepare for,** ríkht-'n zikh

**prescription**, re-tsépt (der)
**(to) press tightly**, kvétsh-'n, drík-'n
**(to) pretend**, mákh-'n an ón-shtel
**pretty**, sheyn
**prick**, shtokh (der)
**priest (in Judaism)** koy'n (der)
**priestly blessing ritual**, dú-khen-en
**(to) print**, drúk-'n
**printer**, drúk-er (der)
**prison**, t'fí-se (di), túr-me (di)
**privilege**, pri-vi-lég-i-ye (di), ze-khí-ye (di)
**privilege seeker**, me-yí-khes (der)
**probably**, mes-tá-me
**(to) produce**, a-róys géb-'n
**profits from the top**, smé-te-ne (di)
**(to) promenade**, shpa-tsír-'n
**promise**, vort (dos)
**proper**, áyn-shten-dik, láy-tish
**proper conduct**, derkh-é-rets
**properly**, be-kóv-ed-ik
**proper way**, bay-láy-t'ns
**prophet**, nó-vi
**prostitute**, kúr-ve (di), náf-ke (di)
**proud**, shtolts
**proverb**, shpríkh-vert-'l (dos)
**(to) provide**, tsú-shtel-'n
**prune**, floym (di)
**Psalms, Book of**, tí-lim
**public**, óy-lem (der)
**(to) publish**, a-róys géb-'n
**pudding**, kú-g'l (der), tsí-mes (der)
**(to) pull**, tsí-yen
**(to) pull the wool over one's eyes**, fír-'n in bod a-ráyn
**pulpit**, bí-me (di)
**pulse**, déy-fek (der)
**punch**, kh'-mál-ye (der), zets (der)
**punctilious in ritual matters**, ópe-ge-hit
**punctual**, pínkt-lekh
**pupil**, tál-mid (der)
**pure**, reyn, ekht

**Purim (Feast of Lots),** pú-rim
**Purim pastry,** hó-men-tash (der)
**purity,** réyn-kayt (di)
**purse,** báy-t'l (dos)
**(to) put on phylacteries,** léyg-'n t'-fí-lin
**(to) putter,** pátsh-k'n

# Q

**(to) quarrel,** tse-kríg-'n zikh
**queen,** mál-ke (di)
**question,** frá-ge (di), ká-she (di)
**quilt,** pé-re-ne (di), kól-di-re (di)

# R

rabbi, rov (der)
rabbinic ordination, smí-khe (di)
radical, róyt-er (der), línk-er, (der)
radish, ré-tekh (der)
rag, shmá-te (di)
rage, kas (der)
rain, ré-g'n (der)
raisin, ró-zhin-ke (di)
ram's horn, shóy-f'r
(to) ransom, óys-leyz-'n
(to) rape, far-g'váld-ik-'n
raw, roy
ready, greyt
really, tá-ke, staytch
(to) rear, der-tsíy-'n, oys-ho-de-v'n
reason, sí-be (di)
(to) receive, ba-kú-men, kríg-'n
reception, ka-bó-les pó-nim (der)
recipe, re-tsépt (der)
recollection, zi-kór-'n
(to) recount, der-tséyl-'n
red, royt
redemption, ge-ú-le (di)
(to) regret, kha-ró-te hób-'n
(to) rehearse, í-ber-kház-er-'n
relative, kó-rev (der)
religious court, bés-din (dos)
religious ecstacy, his-lá-ves
religious functionaries, kley kóy-desh (di)
religious majority (fem.), bas míts-ve
religious majority (masc.), bar míts-ve
religious table songs, z'mí-res (di)
reluctant(ly), on khéy-shek
remainder, resht (der)
remedy, re-fú-e (di)
(to) remember, ge-dénk-'n

**rent,** dí-re gelt (di)
**(to) repeat,** í-ber-khaz-er-'n
**representative,** she-lí-akh (der)
**reprobate,** óys-vorf (der)
**request,** ba-kó-she (di)
**(to) rescue,** rá-te-v'n
**researcher,** fór-sher (der)
**(to) resent,** far-drí-s'n
**(to) reside,** vóyn-en
**residence,** dí-re (di), vóyn-ung (di)
**respect,** dé-rekh é-rets
**response to "hello!",** a-léy-khem shó-l'm
**rest in peace (masc.),** ó-lov-a-sho-l'm
**rest in peace (fem.),** o-léy-o-a-sho-l'm
**(to) retreat,** óp-tret-'n
**return,** tsu-rík
**(to) return,** um-kér-'n
**revenge,** ne-kó-me (di)
**(to) revive,** mín-ter-'n, óyf-mint-er-'n
**rich,** raykh
**rid of,** pót-'r
**right,** rekht, ge-rékht
**righteousness,** tse-dó-ke (di)
**righteous one,** tsá-dik (der)
**rigid,** shtayf
**riot in progress,** es tut zikh op khóy-shek
**ritual bath,** mík-ve (di)
**ritual circumciser,** moyl (der)
**ritual fringed garment,** ar-be-kán-fes (der)
**ritual fringes,** tsí-tses (di)
**ritual of counting days between Passover and Shavuot,** tséyl-'n s'-fí-re
**ritual slaughter,** sh'-khí-te (di)
**ritual slaughterer,** shóy-khet (der)
**river,** taykh (der)
**(to) roam aimlessly,** vál-ger-'n zikh, a-rúm-van-der-'n
**roast,** ge-brót-n's (dos)
**(to) roast,** brót-'n
**robber,** gáz-l'n (der)
**robbery,** ge-zéy-le (di)
**robe,** kha-lát (der)

**roll (baked)**, búl-ke (di)
**roll (flat)**, pléts-'l (dos), b'-yá-li (der)
**room**, tsí-mer (der)
**room and board**, kest (di)
**rooster**, hon (der)
**Rosh Hashanah**, ro-she-shó-ne
**rotten**, far-dórb'n, pas-kúd-ne, far-fóylt
**round**, káy-lekh-dik
**round trip**, a-hin un k'rik
**routine**, shtik (der)
**(to) rule**, pás-ke-nen
**(to) rule on a religious question**, pás-ken-en oyf a sháy-le
**rump**, tó-khes (der)
**(to) run**, lóyf-'n
**rush**, yó-ge-nish (dos)
**rye (grain)**, kor'n (der)

# S

**Sabbath**, shá-bes (der)
**Sabbath afternoon repast**, shó-lesh sú-des
**Sabbath bread**, khá-le (di)
**Sabbath conclusion ritual**, hav-dó-le
**Sabbath day dish**, tshó-l'nt
**Sabbath departure ritual**, me-lá-ve mál-ke (di)
**Sabbath eve**, é-rev shá-bes
**Sabbath hospitality**, kí-dish (der)
**Sabbath sanctification ritual**, kí-dish (der)
**sack**, zak (der), tórb-e (di)
**sacrifice**, kórb-'n (der)
**sad**, ú-me-tik
**sadness**, tróy-er (der)
**sad sack**, shle-míl (der)
**salary**, péy-de (di)
**salt**, zalts (der)
**salvation**, ge-ú-le (di)
**sand**, zamd (der)
**sane**, klor
**sash**, gárt-'l (dos)
**satan**, sót-'n (der)
**sated**, zat
**satisfied**, tsu-fríd-'n
**saucepan**, fénd-'l (dos)
**(to) saunter**, shpa-tsír-'n
**(to) save**, shpór-'n
**(to) say**, zóg-'n
**saying**, shpríkh-vert-'l (dos)
**scalp disease**, pár'-kh (der)
**scapegoat atonement ritual**, shlóg-'n ka-pó-res
**schemer**, dréy-kop (der)
**scholar (Hebraic)**, lám- d'n (der)
**school**, shúl-e (di)
**school for intensive study**, ye-shí-ve (di)
**schoolroom**, khéy-der (der)
**science**, ví-s'n-shaft

144

scientist, fór-sher (der)
(to) scold, a-ráyn-zog-'n, on-zíd'l-en
scolding, (id.) mi-she-béy-rakh (der), zid-ler-áy (dos)
scoundrel, óys-vorf (der)
(to) scratch, kráts-'n
(to) scream, kvítsh-'n
screw, shroyf (der)
screwdriver, shróyf-'n tsí-yer (der)
scroll of the Law, tóy-re (di)
(to) scrutinize, kúk-'n ún-ter di nég-'l
sea, yam (der)
seamstress, shnáy-der-ke (di)
seat, bank (di) plats, (der), ort (dos)
second, ré-ge (di), se-kún-de (di), (ordinal) tsvéy-te (di)
secret, sod (der)
secular, vélt-likh
secure, zíkh-er
seder dessert, a-fi-kóy-men (der)
seder handbook, ha-gó-de (di)
seder question, ma nish-tá-ne
seder song, khad-gád-ye
(to) seduce, far-fír-n
(to) see, zen
seems to me, dakht zikh
seldom, zélt-'n
(to) select, óys-klayb-'n
(to) send, shík-'n
sensitivity, ge-fíl (dos)
separately, ba-zún-der
September, sep-tém-ber
sermon, d'ró-she (di)
servant (masc.), ba-dí-ner (der), m'-shó-res (der)
(to) set (sun), far-géy-'n
settle in Israel, a-lí-ye
settlement (colony), yí-shuv (der)
seven, zí-b'n
seventeen, zí-bi-ts'n
seventy, zí-bi-tsik
several, ét-li-khe
sex, ge-shlékht (dos)

**sexton**, shá-mes (der)
**shadow**, shót-'n (der)
**shady character**, pár'-kh (der), óys-vorf (der)
**(to) shake**, shók-l'n
**shame**, bi-zó-y'n (der), shán-de (di)
**(to) shame**, far-shém-en
**(to) share**, téyl-'n zikh
**(to) share in the profit illegitimately**, óp-lek-'n a bén-d'l
**she**, zi
**shelf**, pó-li-tse (di)
**shepherd**, pas-tukh (der)
**ship**, shif (di)
**shirt**, hemd (dos)
**shmuck**, shmok (der)
**shoddy (goods or business)**, shlak, kha-zer-áy
**shoe**, shukh (der)
**shoelaces**, shúkh-bend-lakh (di)
**shoemaker**, shús-ter (der)
**shofar**, shóy-f'r (der)
**shortcoming**, khe-sór-'n (der)
**(to) shorten**, far-kírts-'n
**shot**, shos (der)
**shots**, shi-se-ráy (dos)
**shoulder**, ák-s'l (der), pléy-tse (di)
**show**, shpil (di)
**(to) show**, váy-z'n, tsáyg-'n
**shower**, shprits (der)
**shrew**, yákh-ne (di), ma-khe-shéy-fe (di), yén-te (di)
**shrouds**, takh-rí-khim (di)
**shy**, shé-mev-dik
**sick**, krank
**side**, zayt (di)
**sigh**, krekhts (der), zifts (der)
**sign (portent)**, sí-men (der)
**(to be) silent**, shváyg-'n
**silver**, zíl-ber (dos)
**simpleton**, yold (der), tam (der)
**sin**, a-véy-re (di), zind (di)
**since**, zayt
**(to) sing**, zíng-en

single (one), éyn-tsig
(to) sink, ún-ter-gey-en, zínk-'n
sister, shvés-ter (di)
(to) sit, zíts-'n
site, plats (der)
situation critical, krí-tish, hált-'n shmol
six, zeks
sixteen, zékh-ts'n
sixty, zékh-tsik
(to) skate, glítsh-'n
skid, glítsh-'n
skilled worker, bal me-ló-khe (der)
skin, hoyt (di)
skull, shár-b'n (der)
skull cap, yár-mil-ke (di)
sky, hím-'l (der)
slander, re-khí-les (dos)
slap, khmál-ye (di), patsh (der), zets (der), frask (der)
(to) slap, pátsh-'n
slattern, shlump (der)
slatternly, tse-krókh-'n
(to) slaughter, shékht-'n
slave, shklaf (der)
slavery, shklaf-e-ráy (dos)
(to) sleep, shlóf'-n, tsu-makh-'n an oyg
sleeping place, ge-lég-er (dos)
sleeve, ár-b'l (der)
sleigh, shlít-'n (der)
slim, shlank
(to) slip, óys-glitsh-'n
slob, shlump (der)
slowly, bís-lekh-vays, pa-mé-lakh
small, kleyn
smaller, klén-er
smart, klug
(to) smell, shmék'-n
smile, shméy-kh'l (der)
(to) smile, shméy-khlen
smoke, róy-akh (der)
(to) smoke, róy-kher-'n

**smokestack,** kóym-en (der)
**snack,** nash (der), í-ber-bays-'n (dos)
**(to) snack,** násh-'n, í-ber-bays-n
**(to) snatch up,** óys-khap-'n
**(to) sneak in,** a-ráyn-gan-ven-en zikh
**(to) sneak up on,** ún-ter-gan-ven-en zikh
**sneaky,** g'-néy-vish
**(to) sneeze,** nís-'n
**snobbish,** ón-ge-bloz-'n
**snooze,** drém'l (der)
**(to) snore,** khróp-'n
**snow,** shney (der)
**so,** a-zóy, nu
**soft,** veykh
**soil,** erd (di)
**solace,** treyst (der)
**sole of shoe or foot,** pe-désh-ve (di)
**so long as,** a-bí
**so long as you have your health,** a-bí ge-zúnt
**someone,** é-mets-er
**something,** é-pes
**son,** zun (der)
**song,** ge-záng (dos), lid (dos), zé-mer (der)
**song and dance routine,** hóts-ke (di)
**son-in-law,** éy-dem (der)
**soon,** bald
**sorrow,** tsar (der)
**(to be) sorry,** far-drís-'n
**soul,** né-fish (der), ne-shó-me (di)
**soup,** zup (di)
**sour,** zóy-er
**sour-faced (one),** far-bí-si-ner (der), kvetsh (der), far-krímt-er (der)
**sour-faced,** far-krímt
**sour pickle,** zóy-er-e ú-ger-ke (di)
**south,** dó-rem
**souvenir,** án-denk (der)
**Spanish–Hebrew folk tongue,** la-dí-no
**(to) spare no effort,** lég-'n zikh in der leng un der breyt
**(to) sparkle,** fínkl-en
**(to) speak,** réd-'n

speaker, réd-ner (der)
(to) speak up, óp-ruf'n zikh
spectator, kí-bi-tser (der)
(to) speculate, trákht-'n, íber-trakht-'n
speech, d'ró-she (di), ré-de (di)
spinach, shpi-nát (der)
spinach soup, shtshav (der)
spine, rú-k'n-beyn (der)
spinster, ál-te moyd (di)
spirit (of the dead that invades the body of the living), dí-bik (der)
(to) spit, shpá-yen
spleen, milts (di)
(to) split one's sides laughing, hált-'n zikh bay di záy-t'n
(to) spoil, kál-ye mákh-'n
spray, shprits (der)
spring, frí-ling (der)
(to) squeak, skríp-'n
(to) squeeze, kvétsh-'n, drík-'n
stage, bí-ne (di)
stairs, trep (di)
(to) stammer, hík-en
(to) stand, shtéy-en
star, shtern (der)
starched, shtayf
Star of David, mó-g'n dó-vid
status, yí-khes (der)
statute, ge-zéts (dos)
(to) stay, bláyb-'n
(to) steal, gán-ven-en, tsú-gan-ven-en
(to) steal away, a-vék-gan-ven-en zikh
(to) steal from, ba-gán-ve-nen
steambath, shvits bod
steps, trip (di)
stick, shték-'n (der)
stiff, shtayf
stingy, karg
(to) stir up, far-mísh-'n
stitch, shtokh (der)
stock, za-pás (der)
stockings, zók-'n (di)

**stomach,** boykh (der), mó-g'n (der)
**stooge,** me-shó-res (der)
**(to) stop,** óyf-her-'n
**store,** krom (der), kleyt (di)
**story,** máy-se (di), ro-man (der)
**story (floor of a building),** shtok (der)
**stove,** óy-v'n (der)
**straight,** glaykh
**strange,** mód-ne
**stranger,** frémd-er (der)
**street,** gas (di)
**streetwalker,** kúr-ve (di), náf-ke (di)
**strength,** ge-vú-re (di), kóy-akh (der)
**(to) stroll,** shpa-tsí-r'n
**strong,** shtark
**stronger,** shtárk-er
**struggle,** kém-f'n
**stubbornness,** ak-shó-nes (dos)
**stubborn one,** ák-sh'n (der)
**student of a yeshive,** ye-shí-ve bókh-'r
**stuffed cabbage,** hó-lib-tses (di)
**stuffed derma,** kísh-ke (di)
**stultification,** láy-tish ge-lékh-ter
**stupid person,** ku (di)
**style,** mó-de (di)
**(to) subvert,** ún-ter-shtel-'n a fís-'l
**(to) succeed,** ge-rót-'n, mats-lí-akh zayn, ge-líng-en
**successful,** máz-'l-dik
**suddenly,** plúts-ling
**(to) suffer,** láyd-'n, óp-ku-men
**(to) suffice,** klék-'n
**sugar,** tsú-ker (der)
**(to) suggest,** fór-leyg-'n
**suitable,** tóyg-'n
**suitcase,** tsha-ma-dán (der)
**suitor,** ka-va-lyér (der), kho-s'n (der)
**summer,** zú-mer (der)
**summer cottage,** kókh-a-leyn (dos)
**sun,** zun (di)
**Sunday,** zún-tik

**sunset (time)**, far-nákht
**sunshine**, zú-nen shayn (di)
**superficial**, óy-ber-flekh-likh
**superstition**, bó-be máy-se (di)
**supply**, za-pás (der)
**support (financial)**, kest (di)
**(to) support**, óyf-halt-'n, óys-halt-'n
**supreme effort**, kríkh-'n oyf á-le fir
**sure**, zíkh-er
**surgeon**, khi-rúrg (der)
**surly**, ón-ge-bloz-n
**(to) surrender**, ún-ter-geb-'n zikh
**survival**, kí-yum (der)
**(to) survive**, óys-halt-'n
**survivor**, léb-'n ge-blib-'n-er (der)
**suspenders**, shláy-kes (di)
**sway in prayer**, shók-l'n zikh
**sweet**, zis
**sweetness**, zís-kayt
**(to) swim**, shvím-en
**swindle**, shvínd-'l (der)
**swine**, khá-z'r (der)
**(to) switch on**, ón-tsind-'n
**sympathetic**, sim-pá-tish
**synagogue**, shul (di)
**synagogue elder**, gá-be (der)

# T

**table**, tish (der)
**tablecloth**, tísh-takh (der)
**tail**, véy-d'l (der)
**tailor**, shnáy-der (der)
**(to) take**, ném-en
**(to) take a cut of the loot**, óp-lek'n a béyn-d'l
**(to) take after**, ge-rót-'n in
**take care**, hit zikh
**(to) take delight in**, kvél-'en
**(to) take off**, óys-ton
**(to) take part**, án-teyl ném-en
**(to) take pleasure**, ha-nó-e hób-'n
**(to) take pride**, shtol-tsír-'n
**(to) take the trouble**, mat-rí-akh zayn
**tale**, ge-shíkh-te (di)
**talented**, féy-ik
**tall**, hoykh
**taste**, tam (der)
**tasty**, ba-támt, ge-shmák
**(to) tattle**, óys-zog-'n
**tavern**, shenk (di)
**tea**, tey (di)
**teacher**, lér-er (der)
**teacher (religious)**, me-lá-med (der)
**teapot**, tsháy-nik (der)
**(to) telephone**, óp-kling-en, op-ruf-'n
**(to) tell**, der-tséyl-en
**(to) tell off**, a-ráyn-zog-'n
**ten**, tsen
**Ten Commandments**, a-sé-res-a-dib-res
**tender**, tsart, veykh
**tense**, ón-ge-tsoy-g'n
**terms (legal)**, ba-díng-ung-en (di)
**terrible**, fe, kha-ló-shes, shrék-lakh
**terrifying**, shrék-lakh
**(to) terrorize**, í-ber-shrek-'n

testicles, béy-tsim (di)
(to) thank, dánk-en
thank God, got tsu dánk-en
thank you, a dank
thankful, dánk-bar
thanksgiving blessing, she-khe-yó-nu
the (fem. sing., also all plurals), di
the (masc. sing.), der
the (neut. sing.), dos
the (plu.), di
their, zéy-er
then, dé-malt
there, ot, dórt-'n
there, a-hín, dórt-'n
therefore, der-fár, der-í-ber
they, zey
thick, ge-díkht
thief, gá-nef (der)
thimble, fín-ger-hut (der)
thin, din, mó-ger, óys-ge-dart
(I) think, dakht zikh
(to) think, klér-'n, trákht-'n
thirst, dursht (der)
thirteen, dráy-ts'n
thirty, dráy-sik
thought, áyn-fal (der)
thousand, tóy-z'nt
thread, fó-dem (der)
(to) threaten, strá-sh'n
three, dray
throat, gór-g'l (der), haldz (der)
through, durkh
(to) throw out, a-róys várf-'n
thumb, grób-er fíng-er (der)
Thursday, dó-ner-shtik
thus, a-zóy
(to) thwart, far-shtér-'n, óys-mayd-'n
ticket, bil-yét (der)
(to) tickle, kits-len
tidings, b'-sú-re (di)

**tie**, kra-vát (der)
**tight**, shmol
**time**, tsayt (di)
**tiny**, píts-'l
**(to) tire**, mú-tsh'n
**tired**, mid
**tit**, tsíts-ke (di)
**to**, tsu
**toast (to life)**, li-khá-yim
**today**, haynt
**together**, in éy-nem, tsu-zá-men
**toilet**, óp-tret (der)
**tomato**, pó-mi-dor (der)
**tomorrow**, mór-g'n (der)
**tongue**, tsung (di)
**tonsils**, mán-d'l'n (di)
**too bad**, far-fál-en
**too late**, far-fál-en
**too much**, tsu
**tooth**, tson
**top**, drey-d'l (dos)
**top**, shpits (der)
**Torah honor**, a-lí-ye (di)
**Torah reader**, bal k'rí-ye (der)
**Torah scroll**, séy-fer tóy-re (der)
**(to) torment**, mútsh-'n
**tormented to excess**, oyś-ge-mutsh-et
**(to) torture**, páy-nik-'n, mútsh-'n
**total**, sakh-hák-'l (der), ún-tersh-te shú-re (di)
**(to) touch**, ón-ri-r'n, tshép-'n
**touching (emotionally)**, rír-'n-dik
**tough guy**, khév-re-man (der) shtárk-er (der)
**town**, shtot (di)
**trade**, fakh (der)
**tradesman**, sóy-kher (der)
**tragedy**, úm-glik (der)
**train**, ban (di)
**(to) translate**, í-ber-zets-'n
**translation**, taytsh (der), í-ber-zéts-ung (di)
**treasure**, óy-tser (der)

**(to) tremble**, tsí-ter-'n
**tricky**, g'-néy-vish
**(to) trip someone**, ún-ter-shtel-en a fís-'l
**trouble**, tsó-re (di)
**(to) trouble**, mú-tsh-'n
**troubles**, ye-sú-rim (di), tsó-res (di)
**trousers**, hóy-z'n (di)
**truth**, é-mes (der)
**(to) try to atone**, zikh shlóg-'n al khet
**Tuesday**, dínst-ik
**tune**, ní-g'n (der)
**turmoil**, i-ber-kér-i-nesh (dos)
**(to) turn around**, úm-ker'n zikh
**twenty**, tśvan-tsik
**two**, tsvey
**type**, sort (der)
**typewriter**, shráyb-ma-shin (di)

# U

ugh, fe
ugly, mis
ugly person or thing, mís-kayt (dos)
umbrella, shí-rem (der)
unbalanced, tse-dráyt
unbecoming, mis
uncle, fé-ter (der)
unclean (dietary), treyf; id., illegal, immoral
uncoordinated, tse-krókh-'n, um-ge-lúmp-ert
undecipherable, kó-tshe-res mit lá-pe-tes
under, ún-ter
underclothes, ún-ter-vesh (dos)
underpants, mát-kes (di)
(to) understand, far-shtéy-en
underwear, gát-kes (di)
(to) undress, óys-ton zikh
uneducated, prost
unemployed, a-rúm-gey-en léy-dig
unfortunately, né-bekh
university, u-ni-ver-si-tét (der)
unkempt, tse-krókh-'n, tse-shóy-bert
unleavened "bread", máts-e (di)
untidy person, shlump (der)
until, biz
until one hundred and twenty, biz hún-dert un tśvan-tsik
up front, óyb-'n on
up (ward), a-róyf
upper crust, p'-néy (di), smé-te-ne (di)
uproar, ta-ra-rám
upset (disturbed), a-rúm-gey-en on a kop
upside down, móy-she ka-póyr
(one who) urinates, písh-er (der)
us, unz
(to) us, undz
useful, tóyg-'n

**(to) use one's assets in sickness,** far-krénk-'n, óys-krenk-'n
**usually,** ge-véynt lekh
**utility,** tákh-lis (der)
**(to) utilize,** óys-nits-'n
**utmost uselessness,** tish un náyn-tsig ka-pó-res

# V

**vacation,** va-ká-tsi-ye (di)
**vaccination,** pók-'n (di)
**vagina,** va-gí-ne (di)
**valuable,** táy-er, vért-ful
**valley,** tol (der)
**vegetable,** grins (dos)
**verdict,** p'sak (der), úr-tel (der)
**very,** gor
**vicarious atonement,** shéyn-e réyn-e ka-pó-re
**victim,** kórb-'n (der), ka-pó-re (di)
**vigor,** kóy-akh (der)
**vilification,** lósh-'n hó-re (dos)
**village,** dorf (der), shtét-'l (dos)
**vinegar,** é-sik (der)
**violent death,** mí-se me-shú-ne (di)
**violin,** fíd-'l (der)
**virgin,** b'sú-le (di)
**virtue,** máy-le (di)
**visiting the sick (act of),** bí-kur khóy-lim
**voice,** shtím-e (di)
**(to) vote,** shtím-en
**vulgar,** bí-lik, ge-méyn, grob, níd-rik
**vulgar person,** dóv-'r ákh-'r (der)

# W

wag, lets (der)
wages, péy-de (di)
(to) wage war, mil-khó-me hált-'n, kémf-'n
wagon, vóg-'n (der)
wagon driver, bal-e-gó-le (der)
(to) wait, várt-'n
(to) wait to be asked, lóz-'n zikh bét-'n
(to) walk, shpa-tśi-r'n
wall, vant (di)
wan, bleykh
(to) want, vél-en
war, mil-khó-me (di)
warm, vá-rem
(to) warn, ón-zog-'n
(to) wash, vásh-'n
wasted, pust un pas
wasteful, a-véy-re (di)
watch, zéy-ger (der)
(to) watch carefully, kúk-'n ún-ter di nég-'l
watchmaker, zéy-ger-makh-er (der)
water, vá-ser (dos)
watermelon, ká-ve-ne (di)
wave, khvál-ye (di)
wealth, a-shí-res (dos)
wealthy, raykh
wealthy man, g'-vír (der), nó-gid (der)
(to) wear, tróg-'n
wedding jester, bád-kh'n (der)
wedding officiant, mi-sá-der ki-dú-shin
Wednesday, mít-vokh
(to) weep, klóg-'n
weeping, ge-véyn (dos)
welfare recipient, me-ká-b'l
well, nu
well said, gut ge-zógt
wet, nas

**what,** vus
**what do you care,** vus art es dikh
**what is the matter with you,** vus iz mit dir
**what is the trouble,** vus iz der mer
**what's up,** vus tut zich
**what time is it,** vi-fíl iz der zéy-ger?
**wheat,** veyts (der)
**wheel,** rud (der)
**when,** az, ven
**whenever,** ven nor
**where does it hurt,** vu tut dir vey
**where to,** vu-hín
**which,** vél-kher
**while,** b'éys
**whim,** ka-príz (der)
**whiskey,** brón-f'n (der), shnaps (der)
**(to) whistle,** fáyf-'n
**white,** vays
**who,** ver
**whole,** gants
**wholeheartedly,** mít-'n gánts-'n hárts-'n
**whom,** vém-en
**why,** far-vús, staytch, va-rúm
**wide open,** héf-ker, fray
**widow,** al-mó-ne (di)
**widower,** ál-men (der)
**wife,** vayb (di)
**wife of landowner,** prí-tse
**wife of wealthy man,** ne-gí-dis-te (di)
**wig (fem.),** shayt-'l (dos)
**wig (masc.),** pa-ruk (der)
**wild,** vild
**will,** tsa-vó-e (di)
**window,** fén-ster (der)
**wing,** flíg-'l (der)
**winter,** vín-ter (der)
**wisdom,** séy-kh'l (der)
**wise person,** khó-khem (der)
**(to) wish,** vél-en
**witch,** makh-e-shéy-fe (di)

**with**, mit, mít-'n
**(to) withdraw**, óp-tret-'n
**withered**, óys-ge-dart, trík-'n
**within**, ín-e-vey-nik
**without**, on
**without a doubt**, on a só-fek
**(one) without visible means of support**, lúft-mensh (der) tróm-be-nik (der)
**witness**, eyd (der)
**woe**, oy-vey
**woman**, froy (di)
**womb**, trakht (di)
**wonder**, vún-der (der)
**(to) wonder**, trákht-'n, vún-der-'n, klér-'n
**wood**, holts (dos)
**woods**, vald (der)
**word**, vort (dos)
**words**, vért-er (di)
**work**, ár-bet (di)
**worker**, ár-bet-'r (der)
**world to come**, é-mes-e velt (die), óy-lem há-be (der)
**wordly**, vélt-likh
**worry**, dáy-ge (di)
**(to) worry**, í-ber-trakht-'n
**worthless thing**, shmek tá-bik (der), gór-nisht mit gór-nisht
**(to be) worthwhile**, lóyn-en, k'-day
**wound**, má-ke (di)
**wringing wet**, fitsh nas
**wrong doing**, shlekht

# Y

**yawn**, géy-nets (der)
**yearn**, bénk-'n
**yellow**, gel
**yesterday**, nékht-'n
**Yiddish**, yí-dish
**Yom Kippur eve**, kol níd-re
**Yom Kippur eve opening liturgy**, kol níd-re
**you (plu.)**, ir
**you (sing., informal)**, du
**you (sing., formal)**, ir
**(to) you**, dikh
**(to) you**, dir
**(to) you (plu. or formal sing.)**, aykh
**you are welcome**, ni-tó far vus
**you must be out of your mind**, frish, ge-zúnt un me-shú-ge
**youngest daughter**, me-zín-ke (di)
**youngest son**, me-zín-ik (der)
**young girl**, méy-d'l (di)
**young man**, bókh-er (der)
**young person**, tsú-tsik (der)
**youngster**, yúng-er (der)
**young upstart**, písh-er (der)
**your (familiar)**, dayn

## JEWISH PROVERBS

a beyze tsung iz erger fun a shlekhter hant.
An angry tongue is worse than an evil hand.

a foyl'n iz gut tsu shik'n noch dem malakhamoves.
Send a lazy man to fetch the Angel of Death.

a groyser oylem un nito kayn mensh.
A big crowd—but not a single human being.

a guter mensh nor der beyzer hunt lost nit tsu tsu im.
He's a fine fellow but his mad dog won't let you near him.

a gut'n helft a vort; a shlekht'n helft afile kayn shteyn oykh nit.
You can correct a decent person with a word; even a stone won't change an evil one.

a halber emes iz a gantzer lig'n.
A half-truth is a whole lie.

a kalyike git men gikher a nedove vi a talmid khokhem.
Cripples get handouts quicker than scholars.

a krank'n fregt men; a gezunt'n git men.
You ask a sick person what he'd like; you serve a healthy one.

a sakh homens nor eyn purim.
There are many Hamans, but only one Purim.

a sheyn ponim kost gelt.
A good appearance costs money.

a shlekhter sholem iz besser fun a gute milkhome.
A poor peace is better than a good war.

a toit'n baveynt men zib'n teg; a naar, dos gantze leb'n.
You mourn seven days for the dead; a lifetime for a fool.

an aynredenish iz erger vi a krenk.
A delusion (fantasy, conceit) is worse than a disease.

az a leyb shloft, lozt men im shlof'n.
Let sleeping lions sleep.

az a nar halt di ku bay di hemer, ken zi a kluger melk'n.
If a fool holds the horns of a cow, it's easy for a wise man to milk her.

az a nar shvaygt vert er oykh gerekhn't ts'vishn di kluge.
When a fool keeps still he, too, is counted among the wise.

az ale kales zaynen sheyn, vu kumen ahin di miese meydlakh?
If all brides are pretty, what happens to the ugly girls?

az der milner shlogt zikh mit'n koymen-kerer vert der milner shvarts un der koimen-kerer vays.
When the miller and the chimney-sweep quarrel, the miller gets black and the chimney-sweep gets white.

az dos meyd'l ken nit tantz'n, zogt zi as di klezmer kenen nit shpil'n.
A girl who can't dance complains that the musicians can't play.

az men hot a nay kleyd'l oyf der vant, iz dos alte k. ₃yd kayn shande nit.
If you've got a new dress, you're not ashamed of the old one.

az men hut gelt iz men i klug, i sheyn, i men ken gut zing'n.
If you have money, you're wise and handsome and can even sing well, too.

az men iz broygez oyf'n khaz'n entfert men nit omeyn?
If you're angry at the cantor, you don't say Amen?

az men khazr't tsu fil iber vi gerekht men iz, vert men umgerekht.
If you protest your innocence too much, you must be guilty.

beser mit a klug'n tsu farlir'n, eyder mit a nar tsu gevinen.
Better to lose with a wise partner than to win with a foolish one.

beser zikh aleyn tsu vinsh'n eyder yenem tsu shelt'n.
Better to wish good things for one's self than to curse others.

ikh zol handlen mit likht, volt di zun nit untergegang'n.
If I sold candles, the sun would never set.

libe is vi puter, s'iz gut mit broyt.
Love is like butter, it goes well with bread.

mit a fraynt iz gut kugel tzu es'n, ober nit fun eyn teler.
It's good to eat kugel with a friend, but not from one plate.

mit fremde hent is gut fayer tsu shar'n.
It's easy to poke the fire with someone else's hands.

orem zayn is kayn shande, ober es iz oykh nit kayn groyser koved.
Poverty is no disgrace, but it's not a great honor either.

fun a karg'n g'vir un a fet'n bok genist men ersht nokh'n toyt.
A rich miser and a fat goat are of no use until they are dead.

eyn nar ken mer freg'n, eyder tsen kluge kenen entfer'n.
One fool can ask more questions than ten wise men can answer.

a gut'n fraynt bakumt men umzist, a soyne muz men zikh koyf'n.
Good friends come free; you buy yourself an enemy.

a gut'n vet der sheynk nit kalye makh'n; a shlekht'n vet der besmedresh nit
farikht'n.
The tavern will not spoil a good man; the synagogue will not help a bad one.

a khesor'n, di kale iz tsu sheyn.
The trouble is the bride is too pretty.

a nar geyt in bod arayn un fargest zikh dos ponim opvash'n.
A fool goes to the bathhouse and forgets to wash his face.

a nar vakst on reg'n.
A fool grows without rain.

a shlemaz'l falt oyf'n ruk'n un tsebrekht zikh di noz.
A born loser falls on his back and breaks his nose.

ale yid'n kenen zayn khazonim, ober meystens zaynen zey heyzerig.
All Jews can be cantors, but for the most part they are hoarse.

az an oriman est a hon iz oder er iz krank oder di hon.
When a pauper eats chicken one of them must be sick.

az di mame ruft dos kind mamzer, meg men ir gloyb'n.
When a mother calls her child a bastard, you can believe her.

az got vil shist a beyzem.
If God wills it, a broom can shoot.

az men lebt on a kheshb'n shtarbt men on takhrikhim.
If you live without a budget, you may die without shrouds.

az men vil a hunt a zets geb'n, gefint men shoyn a shtek'n.
If you really want to hit a dog, you'll find a stick.

got vet helf'n, ober biz er vet helf'n, zol got helf'n.
God will surely help. But until He helps, may God help us.

er iz nit kayn groyser khokhem un nit kayn kleyner nar.
He's no great sage and no small fool.

oyf a fremder bord iz gut zikh tsu lernen sher'n.
It's good to learn to barber on another's beard.

az a shlemaz'l koylet a hon, get er; dreyt er on a zeyger, shteyt er.
When a sad sack kills a hen it keeps moving; when he winds a clock it stops.

## THE BLESSING

lang leb'n zolt ir.
Long life to you.

a brokhe oyf aykh.
May you be blessed.

aza yor oyf mir.
May I have a year as good as . . . (this suit looks on you).

ir zolt fun kayn shlekhts nit vis'n.
May you never know any trouble.

lomir zikh bageygnen oyf simkhes.
May we meet on happy occasions.

zol aykh got tsushik'n vus ir vintsht zikh aleyn.
May God grant you all you wish for yourself.

got zol aykh shoymer un matzil zayn.
May God protect and deliver you.

ir zolt im migad'l zayn tsu toyre, tsu der khupe, un tsu masim toyvim.
May you be privileged to rear him to the study of Torah, to the wedding canopy
    and to the performance of good deeds.

ir zolt im gring ertziyen.
May you rear him easily.

a gezint in dir.
Good health to you.

## . . . AND THE CURSE

in d'rerd arayn.
To hell with it.

gey in d'rerd arayn.
Go to hell.

ver geharget.
Get killed.

'khob im in d'rerd.
To hell with him.

oyskrenk'n zol er di mames milkh.
May his illness consume his mother's milk.

zoll er krenk'n un gedenk'n.
May he suffer and remember.

shrayb'n zol men im retzept'n.
May they write prescriptions for him.

kayn dokter zol em nit kenen helf'n.
May he be beyond the help of any doctor.

oyf doktoyrem zol er es oysgeb'n.
May he spend his money on doctors.

a veytik im in boykh.
A pain in his belly.

a kram in di krizhes.
A cramp in his back.

red'n zol er fun hits.
May he be delirious.

geshvolen un gedrolen zol er ver'n.
May he swell up with varicose veins.

fargelt un fargrint zol er ver'n.
May he turn yellow and green.

a mageyfe un a mab'l zol oyf im kumen.
May he be plagued with an epidemic and a flood.

a kholeriye oyf im.
The cholera take him.

a rikh in zayn tat'n.
To the devil with his father.

a kleyn kind zol nokh im heys'n.
May they name a baby after him.

neyen zol men im takhrikhim.
May they sew shrouds for him.

vos·es hot zikh mir gekholemt di nakht, un yene nakht, un ale nekht zol oysgeyen
tsu zayn kop.
May the nightmares I had last night, and the other night, and all the past nights,
befall him.

got zol im bentsh'n mit dray mensh'n: eyner zol im halt'n, der tsveyter zol im
shpalt'n, der driter zol im behalt'n.
May God bless him with three men: one to hold him, the second to split him,
and the third to bury him.

ver'n zol fun dir a blintse, un fun im a katz, er zol dikh oysfres'n, un mit dir zikh
dervarg'n, volt men fun aykh beyde poter gevor'n.
May you turn into a blintze, and may he turn into a cat, and may he eat you up
and choke on you, so we can be rid of the both of you.

tzen shif'n mit gold zol er farmog'n, un dos gantze gelt zol er farkrenk'n.
May he own ten ships laden with gold and may he spend it all in sickness.

hob'n zol er hundert hayzer, un in yed'r hoyz hundert tzimer'n, un in yed'r
tzimer hundert bet'n, un a kadokhes zol im varf'n fun eyn bet tzum tzevyt'n.
May he own a hundred houses, and in every house a hundred rooms, and in
every room a hundred beds, and may he toss from bed to bed with the plague.

megilg'l zol er ver'n in a henglaykhter, bay tog zol er heng'n, un baynakht zol er
brenen.
May he be reincarnated as a chandelier and hang by day and burn by night.

got zol im helf'n er zol zayn gezunt un shtark un shtendig freyg'n vus far a veter
s'iz in droys'n.
May God help him to be well and strong and always need to ask about the
weather outside.

got zol oyf im onshik'n a nar.
May God plague him with a fool.

aza yor oyf im.
May he have a year as bad as . . . (the trouble he made for me).

## THE SACRED VOCABULARY

a blat gemore.
A page of the Talmud. The *gemore* is one of the two basic components of the
Talmud text.

a maymer khazal.
A saying of our sages, may their memories be for a blessing. The word *khazal* is
an acronym: *kha—khakhomeynu*, our sages; *za—zikhroynom*, their memories;
*li—livrokhe*, be for a blessing.

arbe kanfes.
Four cornered undergarment, with ritual fringes on each corner, worn by pious
males in compliance with the Biblical commandment.

bentsh'n.
To recite Grace after meals.

besmedresh.
Place of study; usually within a synagogue.

brokhe.
Benediction, blessing.

di gemore lern't.
The *gemore* teaches. The traditional way of citing a passage.

der medresh brengt.
The *medresh* brings (raises the question, or amplifies the point).

der rebe geyt zog'n toyre.
The rabbi is about to give his interpretation of some sacred text.

fal'n koyrim.
To fall on one's knees in the liturgical reenactment of the *yom kiper* ritual required of the Temple *koyhanim*, priests. When the Cantor reaches that point
in the service on *yom kiper* where this rite is described, he actually falls to his
knees and bows his head.

fir kashes.
The four questions asked by the youngest at the *seyder* which motivates the retelling of the story of Israel's exodus from Egypt.

firzoger'n.
The woman who read the prayers aloud for the benefit of those in the women's
section of the synagogue who were not able to read the Hebrew.

gabe.
Elder of the synagogue.

gey'n menakh'm ov'l zayn.
To pay a condolence call.

gey'n m'vak'r khoyl'm zayn.
To visit a sick person.

geyn oyf keyver oves.
To visit parents' or grandparents' graves.

gotenyu.
Dear God!

hashgokhe.
Supervision; usually in the context of assuring the *kashrut* of foods.

hashem yisborakh.
Blessed God.  Since a pious Jew will not use the name of God in every day conversation, the word *hashem*, the Name, is used in its place.

krig'n an aliye
To be called to bless the Torah in the synagogue

leyg'n t'filin.
To put on phylacteries.

makh'n a brokhe.
To recite the appropriate benediction.

makh'n a moytsi.
To make the benediction over bread at the beginning of a meal.

makh'n havdole.
To recite the liturgy of farewell to the Sabbath.

makh'n kidish.
To recite the blessings over wine on Sabbaths and festivals.

ton a mitsve.
To perform a good deed.

zog'n kadish.
To recite the Mourners Kaddish at services in the synagogue; to be in mourning.

zog'n tilim.
To recite psalms in behalf of a seriously ill person, or at the coffin of a deceased.

## APHORISMS: THE VINEGAR AND HONEY OF YIDDISH

### Independence

shlekht hob'n a balebos vus iz iber zikh aleyn nit kayn balebos.
Bad to have a master who cannot master himself.

mit ayz'n shmid men dem guf; mit gold di neshome.
The body is conquered with steel; the soul with gold.

gey nisht tsu gast oyb di falst tsu last.
Don't be a guest if you need to be.

a farhayrerter man iz a gefangener vus tsolt kontrebutsie dos gants leb'n.
A husband is a captive who pays tribute all his life.

nisht loz'n zikh onton a yokh iz gringer vi es arunter tsuvarf'n.
Easier to refuse a yoke than to throw it off.

bistu gefalen—heyb zikh aleyn oyf; heyb'n dikh andere oyf, bistu nokh mehr
  gefalen.
When you fall—pick yourself up. If you let others help—you fall lower.


### Old Age

dos ponim fun an alt'n man, iz a landkarte tzum keyver.
An old man's face is a roadmap to the graveyard.

di altkayt shrayt tsu der yugn't: vuhin loyfstu? di yugn't tsu der altkayt: vuhin
  krikhstu?
The aged cannot understand why the young run. The young cannot understand
  why the aged creep.

yugn't zogt shir hashirim, altkayt—kines.
Youth sings the "Song of Songs"; the old, wail "Lamentations."

di vus zenen arop fun der sene vil'n onfir'n hinter der sene.
Those who can no longer play a scene want to direct from backstage.

mir derkenen az mir elter'n zikh ven di yunge hoyb'n on zikh fun unz uptsuruk'n
  un di alte tsutsuruk'n.
We know we're getting old when the young draw away and the old draw near.

der yunger khapt, der mit'lyoriker nemt, der alter khapt arayn.
Youth grabs, middle age takes, old age accepts.

di vus red'n keg'n der shtiferay fun di yunge, vil'n fun der velt makh'n a moyshev z'keynim.
Those that protest against youth's revels, will make the world into a home for the aged.

## Truth

zug'n dem emes veg'n yenem—ken oykh a ligner; farleykenen dem emes veg'n zikh ken oykh an orentlekher mentsh.
A liar may tell the truth about someone else, but even an honest man can lie about himself.

ikh gloyb nit in dem emes fun der libe; ikh gloyb ober in der libe fun emes.
I don't believe in truth in love, but in the love of truth.

ven oyf der velt vult nor geven ayn veg, der veg fun emes, vult er lang shoyn farvaks'n gevor'n.
If truth were the only path in the world, it would be long overgrown.

der veg tsum emes iz oft farshpreyt mit lig'n.
The path to truth is often strewn with lies.

der naketer emes vert oft bakleyt fun ligner.
The naked truth is often dressed by liars.

dem emes darf men zukh'n, vayl dos iz a zakh vus ale behalt'n.
One must search for the truth since everyone tries to hide it.

gib nisht kayn vort dem vos brekht zayn vort.
Don't give your word to one who breaks his word.

der emes iz vi gold; men darf tif grob'n biz men gefint im.
Truth is like gold. You must dig deep to find it.

heystu mir zukh'n dem emes, mistame hostu im farloyr'n.
He who urges others to search for truth must have lost it, himself.

## Farewell

beser avek fun yenem, eyder yener zol avekgeyn fun dir.
Better to leave than to be left.

## Labor

di gringste arbet iz heys'n yenem tzu arbet'n.
The easiest job is to tell someone else to work.

ven du vilst az dayn arbet zol zikh nit farerger'n, trakht shtendik vi ir tsu far-
beser'n.
If you don't want your work to go bad, find ways to improve it.

es vaks'n di mazoles fun di raykhe, oyf di mazolyes fun di oreme.
The fortunes of the rich grow on the callouses of the poor.

s'iz beser arbet'n mit a plan, un der plan iz, az yener zol arbet'n.
It's good to work to a plan, especially if the plan is for someone else to work.

## Poverty

oremkayt iz onshtek'nd, vayl verstu orem, loyf'n fun dir ale.
People run from poverty as if it were contagious.

ven der raykher zeyt dem oriman, trakht er nisht tsu linder'n dem orimans orim-
kayt, nor tsu fargreser'n zayn raykhakayt, vayl er zeyt vi shlekht es iz tsu
zayn an oriman.
When the rich man sees the poverty of the poor, he does not seek to alleviate
their suffering, but to increase his own wealth, since he knows how bad it is
to be poor.

## Honesty

buk'n zikh tzum eyg'l-hazohov tor men nit, ober men muz.
One should not bow to the almighty dollar, but one must.

der gonif iz erlekh ven ganvenen iz shverlekh.
The thief goes straight when there's nothing to steal.

der yoysher fun mentsh'n iz nit mer vi a mentshisher yoysher.
Man's sense of justice is no more than human.

## Insults

baleydik'n ken men mit a vort, oyf iberbet'n zaynen hundert verter oykh veynig.
You can offend with a word, but can't apologize with a hundred.

baleydik'n ken men in yeder tsayt, ober oyf iberbet'n muz men hob'n dem
pasend'n moment.
You can insult any time, but apology takes a special time.

fun baleydik'n geyt men avek mit leydig'n; fun a sh'vakh mit revakh.
Insult, and you walk away empty-handed. Praise and you come away with
profit.

## Boasting

der vus hot lib zikh tsu barimen hot faynt zikh unternemen.
He who loves to boast hates to volunteer.

vilstu zayn dos vos du bist nisht, vestu oykh nisht zayn vos du bist yo.
Try to be what you are not and you end up not being what you are.

barimstu zikh mit dayn emune, hob ikh in dir nisht kayn emune.
Boast of your great faith and I lose my faith in you.

tsu vos zolstu zikh barimen?  sheynkayt zeyt men, klugshaft hert men, gutskayt
    filt men.
Why boast—beauty can be seen, wisdom can be heard, goodness can be felt.

barimen zikh mit shtarkayt iz a shvakhkayt.
To boast of strength is a weakness.


## Pride

ven du varfst arop yenems groyskayt ken men zen vi kleyn du bist.
Man is never smaller than when he is tearing down another.

siz nit sheyn barimen zikh mit dem vus men bazitst, nokh mieser iz tsu barimen
    zikh mit dem vus men bazitst nit.
It's wrong to boast of what you have and worse to boast of what you don't have.

unzer vaytkayt fun mensh'n iz nisht kayn horizontile, nor a vertikale.
The true distances that separate us from each other are vertical, not horizontal.


## Goodness

ven der guter volt nit gevust az er iz gut, volt er nokh beser geven; ven der
    shlekhter volt gevust vi shlekht er iz, volt er azoy shlekht nit geven.
If a good man did not know he was good, he might be even better.  If the evil
    man knew that he was evil, he might not be so evil.

der zoyerer frukht halt zikh shtark oyf'n boym, der ziser falt fun klensten vint'l
    arop.
The bitter fruit holds fast to the branch; the sweet fruit falls in the softest
    breeze.

## Luck

siz beser az men zol dos glik nit zen, eyder zen un nisht kenen derlang'n.
It's better never to see good fortune than to see it and be unable to reach it.

vestu vart'n oyf'n glik, vet dos glik nisht vart'n oyf dir.
Luck will not wait for him who waits for luck.

unzer glik iz, vus der mentsh vil nisht ton alts vus er ken, un ken nisht ton alts
vus er vil.
Our good fortune is that man doesn't do all he can do, and can't do all he wants
to do.

## Money

men ken nit oyfklayb'n kayn gelt ven yener zol dos frier nisht tsevarf'n.
One cannot pick up money that someone else hasn't first scattered.

vert shverer in keshene, vert gringer in harts'n.
Heavy purse, light heart.

gelt neytikt zikh nisht in khokhme, ober khokhme neytikt zikh in gelt.
Money needs no wisdom, but wisdom needs money.

du megst oyb du farmogst.
The answer is yes if you possess.

der mentsh grobt gold; gold bagrobt dem mentsh'n.
Man burrows for gold; gold buries man.

in der toyre shteyt az shoykhed makht blind di zeyendike, ober es iz oykh emes
az shoykhed makht zeyendik di blinde.
The Bible says that a bribe blinds those who see, but it can also make the blind
see.

der klang fun gold iz shtil, ober er hert zikh fun eyn ek velt biz'n tsveyt'n.
Gold rings softly, but is heard around the world.

## Justice

der blinder tor nisht mishpet'n dem zeyendik'n.
The blind should not judge the sighted.

mishpet'n kenen veynik, farmishpet'n ale.
Few can judge; all can condemn.

der rikhter halt fun oynesh, er makht a leb'n derfun.
The judge believes in punishment; he earns a living from it.

## Gratitude

hostu yenem geton a kleyne toyve, un er dankt dir on a shir, vil er mistame du
zolst im ton a gresere.
Endless thanks for small favors only signal future requests for bigger ones.

## Doctors

vert shver in harts'n dem patsient, vert gringer in harts'n dem dokter.
Heavy hearted patients make lighthearted doctors.

S'ken leb'n kranke on doktoyr'm, ober nisht doktoyr'm on kranke.
Patients can live without doctors, but doctors cannot live without patients.

## Subservience

halstu di oyg'n tsu der erd, vestu mer vi verem nisht zen.
When you keep your eyes on the ground, all you can see are worms.

## Marriage

a khasene—a levaye mit klezmorim.
A wedding—a funeral with music.

hostu khasene blind, vet dayn vayb dikh firn bay der noz.
Marry blindly and your wife will lead you by the nose.

der "harey at" iz a kurtser prolog tsu a lange drame.
The wedding vow is a short prologue to a long drama.

di khasene iz a shlos, der get a shlis'l.
Marriage is a padlock; divorce the key.

yunge hob'n khasene fun hits, alte fun kelt.
The young marry because they are hot; the old because they are cold.

vi narish mensh'n zaynen; bagrob'n zey eynem, veynen zey, bagrob'n zey tsvey,
tants'n zey.
How foolish people are—bury one and they cry, bury two and they dance.

**Love**

di levone iz nokh alts der bester shadkh'n.
The moon is still the best matchmaker.

der vus hot alemen lib, iz gelibt fun keynem.
He who loves everyone is loved by no one.

der kush iz oyberflekhlekh; der bis kumt fun tif'n harts'n.
The kiss is superficial; the bite comes from the heart.

hut zikh di libe geendikt hut zi zikh gornisht ungehoyb'n.
If your love affair is over, it never really began.

## LINES FROM MY MOTHER'S LIPS

loz zikh nit shpayen in der kashe.
Don't let anyone spit in your cereal. (Stand up for your rights.)

er hot nit oyf vaser oyf kashe.
He can't even buy enough water for cooking his cereal. (He's broke.)

es ligt im in der linke pyate.
It's lying in his left heel. (It's the last thing on his mind.)

makh'n fun im ash un blote.
Make ashes and mud out of him. (To put one down.)

vus is tsu got iz tsu got; vus iz tsu layt iz tsu layt.
What is God's, is for God, what is man's, is for man. (There are things we owe to God, and things we owe ourselves.)

fun a khaz'r a hor iz oykh gut.
Even a hair from a swine is worth something.

az men est khaz'r zol rinen fun di lip'n.
If you're going to eat swine, let it run over the lips. (If you are going to do something improper, you might as well go all the way.)

m'darf im vi a finfter rud tzum vog'n.
He's about as useful as a fifth wheel on a wagon.

kenen di kleyne oysiyes.
To know the fine print. (To be a scholar or a learned person.)

es iz vert di bobes yerishe.
It's worth my grandmother's legacy. (Nothing.)

strashe di genz.
Go threaten the geese.

tzvey meys'm gey'n tantz'n.
Two corpses about to dance. (Two incompetents about to try something beyond them.)

makh'n shabes far zikh.
To make Sabbath for one's self. (To go it alone.)

farshvarts'n dos ponim.
To blacken one's face. (To be disgraced.)

raykh vi koyrakh.
As rich as Korah (Korah was the Biblical rich man who rebelled against Moses in the desert.)

leyg'n zikh feygelakh in bizem.
To place little birds in one's bosom. (To make impractical plans; to dream impossible dreams.)

klug vi di velt.
As wise as the world.

shlog'n kop in vant.
To bang one's head against the wall. (To insist on doing the impossible.)

reyd'n tsu der vant.
To talk to the wall. (A waste of breath.)

der tate mit di beyner.
Father, down to his bones. (The image of his father.)

mit im iz gut kug'l tsu ess'n.
It's good to eat kugel with him. (Don't count on him in an emergency.)

der biterer trop'n.
The bitter drop. (Euphemism for whiskey.)

dos telerel fun him'l.
The plate from heaven. (Expresses the utmost devotion, i.e., He would get her a plate from heaven; the moon and the stars.)

tseteyl'n oyf zib'n telerlakh.
To apportion something out on seven saucers. (To make a big show of very
  little.)

lek'n honik.
To lick honey. (To strike it rich.)

megst zikh shemen in dayn vayt'n halz.
You should blush deep down to your neck.

do ligt der hunt bagrob'n.
Here is where the dog is buried. (There's the problem.)

drayen a spodik.
To twirl a fur hat. (To pester, annoy, bore.)

der shlimaz'l folgt im nokh.
Bad luck follows his every step.

di shikse baym rov ken oykh paskenen a shayle.
The gentile servant girl in the rabbi's house can also decide on ritual questions.
  (An expression of derision aimed at anyone who attempts to give opinions on
  matters in which he has no competence.)

got di neshome shuldik.
He feels he owes God for his soul. (An overly humble person; a person who
  works hard at appearing innocent.)

leb'n vi got in odes.
To live as God in Odessa. (To live it up.)

fir'n in bod arayn.
To lead one to the bathhouse. (To con someone.)

oplek'n a beynd'l.
To get a lick at a bone. (To share, illicitly, in the profits.)

mit ale pitshevkes.
To the last detail.

dos eybershte fun shteys'l.
From the top of the mortar. (Nothing but the best; the cream of the crop.)

mishteyns gezogt.
Unfortunately, alas.

oyfshtey'n oyf der linker zayt.
To get up on the left (wrong) side.

dergey'n di yor'n.
To annoy unto death.

zol mayns ibergeyen
Let mine pass.

helf'n vi a toyt'n bankes.
It will help like applying cups to a corpse.

ongeton in esik un in honik.
Dressed in vinegar and honey. (All dressed up.)

araynfalen in a shmaltzgrib.
To fall into a pit of chicken fat. (To get lucky.)

zi vert di kapore far im.
She would be his pre-Yom Kippur sacrificial bird. (She's crazy about him.)

es past vi an arbes tsu der vant.
It fits like a pea to a wall. (The height of inappropriateness.)

er makht zikh khaz'r fis'l kosher.
He pretends that pig's foot is kosher. (He pretends he is completely innocent.)

ich vel im geb'n a kadokhes.
I'll give him convulsions. (He won't get one red cent.)

es hut mayn bobes tam.
It has my grandmother's taste. (Terrible!)

gey shray chay vekayom.
Go scream: Living and Eternal God. (Nothing further can be done.)